HOPE, INTOLERANCE, AND GREED

HOPE, INTOLERANCE, AND GREED

A Reality Check for Teachers

Debra J. Anderson, Robert L. Major,
and Richard R. Mitchell

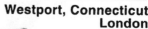

Westport, Connecticut
London

Library of Congress Cataloging-in-Publication Data

Anderson, Debra J. (Debra Jean)
      Hope, intolerance, and greed : a reality check for teachers /
    Debra J. Anderson, Robert L. Major, and Richard R. Mitchell.
          p.   cm.
      Includes bibliographical references and index.
      ISBN 0–275–94821–8 (alk. paper)
          1. Teachers—United States. 2. Education—United States—
    Curricula. 3. Education—Social aspects—United States. 4. Moral
    education—United States. 5. Toleration—Study and teaching.
    I. Major, Robert L. II. Mitchell, Richard R.
    III. Title.
    LB1775.2.A53   1995
    370'.973—dc20   94–32924

British Library Cataloguing in Publication Data is available.

Library of Congress Catalog Card Number: 94–32924
ISBN: 0–275–94821-8

First published in 1995

Praeger Publishers, 88 Post Road West, Westport, CT 06881
An imprint of Greenwood Publishing Group, Inc.

Printed in the United States of America

The paper used in this book complies with the
Permanent Paper Standard issued by the National
Information Standards Organization (Z39.48–1984).

10 9 8 7 6 5 4 3 2

Copyright Acknowledgments

The authors and publisher gratefully acknowledge permission to reprint the following
copyrighted material:

Extracts from Marksjarves, G. (1978, November 7). Elderly poor face inflation and loneliness: A reaction to the question asked by all American city judges—"Do you have any poor
people and, if so, what do you do with them?" *The Free Press*, p. 10.

Every reasonable effort has been made to trace the owners of copyright materials in this
book, but in some instances this has proven impossible. The authors and publisher will be
glad to receive information leading to more complete acknowledgments in subsequent
printings of the book and in the meantime extend apologies for any omissions.

To America's greatest source of hope
its teachers

Contents

Preface

We have the freedom to choose between evil and good, between suicide and life, between hate and love, between immediate gratification and long-range goals. If we wish, we can opt for the cynical, pessimistic view of this world. Or we can take the position of hope, which is stubborn enough to believe that the best is yet to be. That choice—that choice of attitude—is ours. (McGinnis, 1990, p. 159)

America is a great country. Listing its many positive attributes would be impossible. But in some ways America today is in worse shape than it was when the rioting in Watts occurred in 1965. Changes hoped for then materialized only ephemerally.

Greed and blind intolerance still exist; racial hatred is still alive and well; success continues to be measured by addresses, automobiles, and wealth, not by one's character; and hope held by those at the very bottom has been leveled if not extinguished. Nearly thirty years after the first rioting in Los Angeles, "welfare dependency, homelessness, substance abuse, family disintegration, the intergenerational transmission of poverty, teenage pregnancy, illegitimacy, sexually transmitted diseases, . . . violence and other crimes are all worse" (Will, 1993, April 15, p. 26A).

Brazen predators, employed as full-time criminals, stalk nearly every American community; aggressive panhandlers, in obvious need of medical care, tug on people's clothes and demand money; adolescents think it a virtue to avoid success in school; swindlers use charity scams to steal life savings; motorists halted in traffic are dragged from their cars, robbed, beaten, and sometimes shot; and kick-burglars, *wanting* their victims to be at home, smash in front doors and terrorize the occupants into telling them the whereabouts of valuables ("Muggers attack women," 1992; "FBI may try," 1992; Turque, 1992; "Police say huge," 1993; "$50,000 lost in," 1993; Bonner, 1994). At a time when citizens are living longer and more can afford to visit places only dreamed about, they hesitate, fearing it unsafe to do so.

America has so very much going for it, but when even a small minority of its citizens are robbed of their dignity, or feel most look upon them as being inferior, or feel shut out, or are subjected to events instilling fear, something is wrong.

America can be a better place for *all*; it can be everything it is capable of becoming, all that our ancestors dreamed, all that our country's millions of immigrants thought it would be; but to be such, it cannot continue with business as usual.

Educators, our country needs your courage, guidance, and stability. Your help is needed now! You need to expose myths, rethink the curriculum, set high expectations, stop being afraid to discipline children, teach students to be more accepting of those whose only "crime" is to be different, and help Americans put into perspective those things about which they can be hopeful.

At some point in their careers most professionals feel overwhelmed as they realize how little they know and how much more there is yet to learn. But educators must not allow such realities to keep them from being the positive role models today's youth so desperately need.

Educators must never forget that teachers and education are, and always will be, some students' *only* hope. Educators must never forget that they influence every lawmaker and every lawbreaker, and if they handle each in the right way, at the right time, changes lasting a lifetime can happen in an instant.

Hope, Intolerance, and Greed: A Reality Check for Teachers, written by experienced teacher-educators whose privilege it is to work in urban, suburban, and rural K–12 schools each week, is a book about hope and about present and future reality. Its mission is to encourage teachers to see America as it really is and to urge them to reexamine assumptions and to question the status quo. It asks teachers to envision America's becoming a "home" for every citizen and invites them to rediscover their power to influence our country's direction for generations to come. It asks educators always to remember that they are and will remain America's greatest source of hope.

Part One

*Acknowledging Current Realities
and Empowering Teachers through
Professional Development
and the Curriculum*

1

Tolerance and Intolerance

In 1982 Cook County Hospital's trauma unit treated "only" 500 persons who had been shot, and "only" 5 percent of them had been hit by more than one bullet. In 1991 the unit treated about 1,000 gunshot victims and 25 percent had absorbed more than one bullet. (Will, 1993, March 28, p. 23A)

As a society we are too tolerant of some behaviors and too intolerant of others. Chapter 1 addresses this issue and suggests what educators might teach new teachers about tolerance and intolerance.

TOLERANCE

We are learning to live with hate crime, shooting sprees, mindless destructiveness, "I want it so I think I'll take it" attitudes, and many other acts that deny the rights of others.

Church services once enjoyed at night are now scheduled during daylight hours; some high school football games are now played in the afternoon; and travelers using Amtrak or Greyhound are reluctant to venture from the depot. Random acts of violence are everywhere—zoos, shopping-malls, movie theaters, playgrounds, swimming pools. Some even go so far as to say, as does Jesse Jackson, that crimes, especially those against blacks, are becoming unalarming and even acceptable (Jackson, 1990). Benumbed Americans are simply tuning out reality (Mischke, 1993; Powell, 1993;

McGrory, 1993; "As violence in," 1993; "Megamall shooting shatters," 1993; Seib, 1993).

It is impossible to read any newspaper, any day, without learning that a pizza delivery person has been shot or that a cab driver has been stabbed or that a motorist has been pelted with stones or worse. Older persons cannot pull their automobiles into their own driveways after dark without being assaulted and robbed, and kick-burglaries ("kick-burglars typically pick a house where people are home, kick in the doors, and rob, terrorize and sometimes rape the residents" [Potok, 1994, p. 3A]) have become a preferred form of attack (Diaz, 1992; Wangstad, 1992; "Sniper, rock attacks," 1992; "Shots apparently fired," 1992; Finken, 1993).

Rings of thieves stalk our national parks, seashores, and recreational areas. Park rangers call them "car clouts." Knowing tourists often do not carry all of their cash and valuables on their person, these thieves smash vehicle windows and grab cameras, binoculars, suitcases, contents of glove compartments, or anything they can carry ("Thieves ruining vacations," 1991; Healy, 1994). Marauding gangs randomly slash people with razors, stab them with long hat pins, or beat them senseless with golf clubs ("Actress slashed," 1990; "Ten teenage girls," 1989; "Police hold 5," 1987). Armed intruders interrupt church services, rob the worshippers, beat and humiliate the pastor, and ridicule the church members ("Robbers hit church," 1992). Unconscious, dying patients in hospitals have their wedding bands stolen from their fingers (Greene, 1991). Jewelry is taken from bodies that lie in state at local churches ("Jewelry stolen from," 1991). Even our Vietnam Veterans Memorial in Washington, D.C., has had an eight-inch swastika scratched onto two of its granite panels ("Donations to repair," 1988). Ulysses S. Grant's and his wife's tomb gets cleaned up only to be carved upon and spray-painted almost immediately (Sullaway, 1992). People hearing voices telling them "to dig up Abraham Lincoln's body and place it in their bathtub" go into restaurants and kill people because it's "payback time" ("Friend: McDonald's killer," 1993). And purses hung on the inside of public restroom booths are stolen by those who reach over the doors, take the purses, and flee (Bombeck, 1992, November 8). Americans have become too tolerant of uncivilized behaviors!

Perhaps worse, we have allowed others to make us feel guilty when we *are* robbed or otherwise violated. "Warnings to the wise" have become all too familiar. "Lock your vehicle and park it in a well-lighted area." "Do not walk alone, call for an escort." "Give yourself an escape route by leaving space between your car and another vehicle while stopped at a red light."

What if we are raped while walking alone or have our car stolen when we omit locking it or are beaten because we forget to leave ourselves an avenue of escape when stopped at a red light? What if we are involved in a "bump and rob" or a "swoop and squat" automobile robbery? Are we met with sincere empathy and compassion? No! We are thought of as naive and careless. We, the law-abiding, are made to feel responsible for being violated.

If we continue to tolerate vehicle-jackings at our interstate rest areas, the stealing of camping equipment from our parks, and random shootings on our highways, "our country won't be much worth living in" (Greene, 1992, September 24, p. 5).

Although we are too tolerant of some behaviors, we are at the same time too intolerant of others.

INTOLERANCE

Homosexuals, AIDS victims, people seeking and performing abortions, the homeless, food stamp recipients, minorities, non-Christians, women, and the working poor, all have felt the hurtful, often dehumanizing, effects of bias.

Homophobia and fear paralyze church congregations to a point where they exclude AIDS victims ("Priest quits," 1992). Some church congregations accepting homosexuals as members have their church expelled from the denomination ("Baptists say ouster," 1992). Funerals of AIDS victims are picketed by religious leaders who believe funerals for such people glorify a deviant lifestyle (Fruhling, 1992). Employees at health centers performing abortions are stalked and occasionally shot (Rasmussen, 1992; "Wichita abortion doctor," 1993). And some fans of teams playing schools with Jewish students chant anti-Semitic taunts such as "We are Christians, how about you?" throw bagels, and raise their hands in Nazi-style salutes ("Students disciplined for," 1993; Diaz, 1993, March 8, p. 1B). "Somehow during the '80s, decency became a quaint, old-fashioned notion" (Pitts, 1993, p. 13B).

Some hate their fellow human beings simply because they look and think differently. Such hating is akin to burning books just because we do not like their titles.

In light of the intolerance that surrounds us and the reality that Americans accept crime as routine, what should those who are our best hope for the future be taught about tolerance and intolerance?

WHAT BEGINNING TEACHERS NEED TO KNOW ABOUT TOLERANCE AND INTOLERANCE

• We should teach beginning teachers that schools cannot be valuefree and that teachers must fill the growing moral vacuum by helping children understand the difference between right and wrong.

Beginning teachers need to know that despite the diversity in our society, a common core of values that transcends cultural, religious, and socioeconomic differences does exist (Abrams, 1993). Caring, trust, respect, a sense of responsibility—these are values every ideological group can accept, even if they only practice them within their own closely knit group.

• We should teach that today there are more Muslims in the United States than either Congregationalists or Episcopalians (Eck, 1992), and more nonbelievers than in all three groups combined. We are a diverse society in ways that cannot be readily observed.

• We need to teach beginning teachers that by 1995 one-third of our public school children will be members of a minority group ("Study: Public schools," 1991), that Latinos will eclipse blacks as the nation's largest minority group in the year 2010, and that by 2050 only 52.5 percent of Americans will be white ("Hispanics will soon," 1993).

• We need to teach that millions of Americans have never attained the good life, that more than one in ten Americans uses food stamps, and that food banks and soup kitchens in the United States serve 20 million people every month ("Food stamp participation," 1992; "Oxfam: There's hunger," 1992).

• We need to teach educators to recognize their own areas of ignorance and to fill holes in their intellectual dikes. For example, they need to be sensitive to the fact that "immigrants from different countries usually have little contact with one another. They often can't pronounce one anothers' names or read the signs on one anothers' stores: they are baffled by one anothers' foods and have trouble understanding one anothers' English." In Los Angeles, during the 1992 riots, "at the same place where White trucker Reginald Denny was attacked, Takao Hirata, a Japanese-American born behind barbed wire in a World War II internment camp, was nearly killed by a mob shouting anti-Korean epithets" (Moffat, 1992, p. 2A).

• We should teach that one out of every two marriages ends in divorce, and when hearing of a divorce, teachers should not automatically react negatively. Divorce is not *always* a tragedy. Some children are better off not having to hear constant fighting; some may even receive more quality time with each parent. Some single-parent families are, in fact, "intact single-parent families." They are not broken and they are not on crutches. The children in them are not "children of divorce" but, rather, are children who have two parents no longer living together (Goodman, 1988). Every two-parent family and every single-parent family want their children "to read, to write, to learn discipline and proper work habits and how to cooperate and work with others . . . to be participating citizens" (Hentoff, 1993, p. 48A).

• We should teach beginning teachers about maturity and fanaticism. We should teach that fanatics are afraid of pluralism and diversity, abhor learning, have answers instead of questions, certainties in place of hesitations, and minimize or exclude all ideas that confront their own convictions (Wiesel, 1992).

• About maturity we should teach that mature persons do not see everything as white and black, right or wrong, but see all sides of an issue; they place little value upon appearances or first impressions; and they control their self-pity and realize that others have problems and griefs as serious as their own. Mature persons are able to see human frailty not as a betrayal but as a reality of life (Major, 1990).

• We should teach that when we see a person using food stamps and are tempted to be judgmental, we should recall that our government gives nearly 20 billion dollars in farm subsidies each year to our country's 2.2 million farmers and that 40 percent of these payments flow to the wealthiest 60,000 farmers (Goodgame, 1990). We should also recall that the "haves" can write off, on their income tax, interest on their mortgage, interest on their second mortgage, and even interest on their second home. Whether it be in the form of tax breaks or student loans or public assistance, nearly every American receives welfare! The main difference between the welfare flowing to the majority and the welfare the working poor receive is that the majority are given far more and are not demeaned in the process (i.e., by being forced to use different money when purchasing food).

• We should teach beginning teachers that there are good and bad individuals in every group, and that when they encounter misbehaviors, especially juvenile misbehavior—unless vicious beyond the bounds of civility—they should put such misbehavior into perspective. They should visualize Princeton University students running naked across town during their annual "Nude Olympics" (" 'Nude Olympians' spared," 1992), remember that in the college town of LaCrosse, Wisconsin, violence breaks out nearly every year after their annual canoe race ("Violence erupts after," 1991), and remind themselves that college students during spring break do sometimes misbehave ("Youths go on," 1986; "Beach mob torches," 1986).

To put juvenile misbehavior into a more personal perspective, beginning teachers need to remember that 80 percent to 90 percent of all American students commit crimes for which they could be arrested. (Hawkins & Doueck, 1984). Thus they themselves might well be fortunate to have escaped adolescence without a police record. There are double standards in every society, and when we see them at home, we should point them out to all who will listen.

• We should teach that every student has the right to attend school without fear of violence, and that if necessary, disruptive students should be excused from schools so those who want to learn can do so. When expulsions occur, however, teachers must be quick to encourage the establishment of alternative schools and be receptive to developing workable strategies for allowing students to *earn* their way back into school.

• We should teach beginning teachers to respect all honest labor in our workforce regardless of its nature and to honor human beings simply because they work. "Only respect for work itself will undermine the ghetto pathology of 'rich or nothing,' in which low-wage workers are scorned as chumps and suckers, in which the only mainstream life worth living seems to take more money than can be legitimately earned" (Kaus, 1992, p. 139). We should teach that principled, good people with human feelings are present in every occupation. James Alan McPherson calls them "decents" (Harrington, 1992). Human beings do not need to wear suits to work to be "successful." A business suit is not the sine qua non of human dignity. Success comes in varied shapes and colors, not all of them numbered bits of green paper. No group has a monopoly on virtue.

Perhaps dinner conversations regarding the relative prestige of universities and which suburbs have the best reputations, coupled with witty comments about community college graduates and those living in trailer parks, have made us less accepting of people who struggle in life.

• We need to teach teachers to encourage and support lawmakers who have the courage to wipe unneeded, unenforced, and unsupported laws from the books (e.g., laws regarding sodomy, fornication, and adultery). We survive as a country because laws are respected by the majority. But when unenforceable and unnecessary laws are retained and reasonable laws go unenforced, respect for all laws diminishes.

• We should teach beginning teachers to acknowledge that a crime problem exists, but to remind themselves that much of it is caused by repeat offenders whom society has chosen not to try to rehabilitate. An example of the repeat offender is New Yorker Larry Hogue, a fifty-two-year-old homeless crack addict. Hogue roams the streets of the Upper West Side, carries an assortment of weapons—including a machete, a screwdriver, and an ice pick—pursues pedestrians, pulls his pants down, tries to open car doors, and pushes people into traffic; he has been arrested or sent to mental hospitals thirty-seven times since 1985. "But when he gets out, he always returns to the neighborhood" (Greene, 1992, September 8, p. 5).

• We should teach that there are some behaviors for which civilized societies should have zero tolerance. We can understand them, but we do not need to accept them. Some people are simply out of control—they need, for their own sake, to be placed in a structured environment so those with special training might help them.

• We should teach beginning teachers that less than 10 percent of our population causes the vast majority of the problems (*Violent schools, safe,* 1978). But because each individual within this 10 percent commits dozens, sometimes hundreds and even thousands of crimes, our distrust is understandably magnified. We have allowed a small group to unduly influence all of our behavior ("254 crack abusers," 1989; "One in 55," 1987; "Police link suspect," 1987).

It is true, of course, that we are all vulnerable to the excesses of the few—at any time, in any part of the country—and that "it is the disturbing truth that no city, no town, no neighborhood has been spared this bloody plague" ("National killing epidemic," 1992, p. 8); but it is also true that in a democracy the rule of law is the basis of civilization as we know it. In a democracy persons or groups do not have the right to disregard the rights of others.

• We should teach that any crime that robs us of our innocence, takes advantage of our kindness, or preys upon us because we are a caring people should carry greater prison sentences and stiffer fines because persons who have their innocence or spontaneity stolen are never the same. Never again will they share their unhardened, uninhibited giving, even with those most close to them.

An example of the stolen innocence of which we are talking is this: On a cold January evening a New Jersey motorist stopped to help an abandoned crying baby dressed only in a diaper and nightshirt. The baby was sitting in the middle of a deserted road. When the motorist stopped to help, two men rushed from the bushes, put a knife to her throat, stole $300 from her purse, and then fled with the child ("Motorist helping abandoned," 1968). We must never allow those few who hold only contempt for civility to create an America where we are afraid to reach out to someone in need. In Kissimmee, Florida, Tammy George witnessed the execution-style shooting of her boyfriend and two friends and was trying to flag down passing motorists so she could hitch a ride to the police station, but no one would stop to help ("Car jacking survivor recalls," 1992). We do not want to become callous to a point where fear and selfishness are the norm.

• We need to teach that today "whites are bombarded with so many negative TV images and anecdotes of the black underclass that too many have stopped making distinctions among blacks" (Zuckerman, 1991, p. 92). Too many have come to see race first and the individual second; too many "see race explaining black behavior when the explanation often lies somewhere else entirely" (Harrington, 1992, p. 236).

When teachers hear that 56 percent of Baltimore's black males between the ages of eighteen and thirty-five are locked up, are on probation, on parole, out on bond, or are being sought on arrest warrants, they need to remember that "only 8 percent of Baltimore's arrests in 1991 were for violent crimes." Teachers also need to remember that according to the National Institute on Drug Abuse, "77 percent of drug users are white, 15 percent black, 8 percent Hispanic—roughly proportionate to their incidence in the population" (Raspberry, 1993, January 4, p. 81). They also need to remind themselves that the connection between poverty and crime has long been noted. "Today almost 45 percent of all African-American children grow up below the official poverty line, compared to only 16 percent of all white youngsters" (Constitutional Rights Foundation, 1992, p. 6). White persons living under the same disabilities as blacks exhibit similar crime ratios (Tenenbaum, 1947). Myths and stereotypes must be exposed each time they are encountered.

• We should teach that what seems to be a hopeless situation is not. It is not hopeless because teachers have the power to re-create an America that can be everything it is capable of becoming, all that our ancestors dreamed, and all that our millions of immigrants thought it would be.

• We should teach that every educator still has within herself or himself the idealism that brought her or him into teaching in the first place, and that this idealism can be rekindled.

• Finally, we should remind teachers that they have early access to every future judge, newscaster, senator, film producer, movie mogul, and editor; that they interact with every soon-to-be influential person in our country; and that they *can* turn our nation around! By making sure that everyone understands the vital role "certainty of apprehension" plays in deterring crime; by ensuring that everyone understands that to be effective punishments must be perceived by the offenders as punishments; and by helping everyone understand the importance of making drug treatment available for those needing it, teachers can arrest the trend of allowing a small group of the "big and brutal" to control the "small and weak" (Anderson, Mayor, & Mitchell, 1993).

In closing, we empathize with those who believe our society is out of control, and we hear those who feel that our society is in a self-destructive free-fall. We also share the fears of those who believe too many Americans are indifferent to the fact that the United States has been given no guarantee of survival.

Along with them we realize that nine-year-olds steal cars and ram the police cruisers that try to apprehend them ("Newark, NJ, the juvenile," 1992); that seven- and eight-year-olds rape kindergarten students on school buses ("Boys accused of," 1992); and that ten- and twelve-year-olds rob nine-year-old girls at gun point ("Boys use gun," 1988).

And together with them we ask: Are we "raising a generation of young males who measure their manhood by the caliber of their gun and by the number of children they have fathered—a generation for whom camaraderie of a gang has replaced the love of family? (Taylor, 1992, p. 21A).

IMPLICATIONS FOR EDUCATORS

Educators, your help is needed now, more than at any other time in our over 200 years as a nation. Our country needs your guidance, your courage, and your stability. You know what's appropriate and what isn't; what society can tolerate and what it cannot; which behaviors are normal and which won't be outgrown; which cruel actions are deliberate and which are just thoughtless. Trust your feelings and act on them. Your assessment of a student's behavior is still the most significant long-range predictor for determining whether a student will adjust socially or become delinquent (Major, 1990, pp. 91–92).

Society has entrusted you with discovering, teaching, and enforcing the standards necessary for a civilized society to survive. That is your charge, that is your responsibility , and that is why your job is, and will continue to be, our nation's most important. "Surely a tired woman on her way to work at six in the morning on a subway deserves the right to get there safely. Surely it's true that everyone who changes his or her life because of crime—from those afraid to go out at night to those afraid to walk in the parks they pay for—surely these people have been denied a basic civil right" ("President Bush calls," 1992, p. 1). Teachers, please help America restore its foundations of civility and decency.

2 _____

Rethinking the Curriculum:
What America Needs to Learn

> What a wise parent would desire for his own children, that a nation, in so far as it is wise must desire for all children. Educational equality consists in securing it for them. (Tawney, 1931, p. 146)

Are the educational goals we endorse appropriate? Is our curriculum fulfilling the purposes for which it was designed? What attitudes and understandings do we want our students to assimilate before they graduate? What do students need to learn?

Questions such as these are the very core of curriculum development. They are the questions national commissions and task forces address each year.

THE NEED FOR RETHINKING THE CURRICULUM

The dilemmas of curriculum development always remain the same, of course. They concern choice and lack of time. In education, teachers are always "robbing Peter to pay Paul." Teaching one thing well leaves only time to teach something else superficially. Consequently, in the area of curriculum planning, judgments regarding what *not* to teach become as important as what *to* teach.

Has the pendulum swung too far in one direction or the other? Has the delicate balance within our curriculum lost its equilibrium? Should we be teaching some things we are not?

In light of the facts that "83% of all Americans will be victims of a violent crime at least once in their lives" (Kramer, 1992, p. 41), that prison populations have tripled since 1973 (McCarthy, 1993, April 26), that *rural* crime has increased more than 500 percent during the past twenty-five years and will continue to increase (primarily because larger cities are "target hardening," that is, putting up extra lights in areas where high numbers of crimes are reported, cutting down shrubs where rapes have occurred, etc.), perhaps it is time for our schools to teach what is best for our society ("Big-city crime goes," 1993).

This is hardly a unique idea, of course. In 1859 Herbert Spencer, concerned about the needs of *both* the individual and the society, wrote a forty-two-page essay entitled "What Knowledge Is of Most Worth?" In it he postulated that students need "preparation in five realms of activities: (1) direct self-preservation; (2) indirect self-preservation (e.g., securing food, shelter, earning a living, etc.); (3) parenthood; (4) citizenship, and (5) leisure activities" (Ornstein & Hunkins, 1988, p. 146). Everything in the curriculum, he felt, should relate to these five areas. He expected schools to contribute to the general good of the individual *and* to the general good of society. Has our curriculum gotten out of balance?

Spencer did not provide an abundance of examples about what would be taught, but in the area of *direct self-preservation* he would have taught students not to eat wild berries and mushrooms without inspecting them thoroughly because some colorful plants are poisonous. Today he might well support the idea of teaching students how to get under their desks quickly when hearing gun shots.

In the area of *indirect self-preservation*, Spencer most likely would have encouraged students to discover a job that would fulfill them. He would also have taught the skills needed to get and to keep that job. He believed, as did John Dewey fifty years later, that "to find out what one is fitted to do and to secure an opportunity to do it is the key to happiness" (Dewey, 1916, p. 360).

Today Spencer would probably teach the importance of getting up on time, getting to work on time, controlling one's temper, accepting feedback, having realistic expectations, resolving conflict productively, and developing a positive attitude.

Spencer's third realm of activity dealt with *parenthood*. Spencer would probably have taught that the most important job in the world is parenthood. Today he might echo newspaper columnist Mike Royko, who argues, only half in jest, that some parents cannot control their children because they cannot control themselves and should not be raising a Chia pet much less a child (Royko, 1993, March 26, p. 5).

In his fourth area, *citizenship*, Spencer might have taught students something as simple as reporting complaints to the proper authorities. Today he might use air bags as an example. Air bags in motor vehicles, he would teach, have killed and impaired motorists, but the National Highway Safety Administration *cannot* investigate. They cannot because only 544 complaints have been reported, and the agency cannot investigate until they receive 25 complaints per 100,000 cars of a single make and model. So reporting, he would argue, especially in the case of air bags, is not just important to you, it is vital to everyone ("Agency can't investigate," 1992).

In his fifth realm of activity, *leisure*, Spencer might teach students how to listen and how to ask questions. He would because much of our leisure time is spent interacting with people, and because how much we gain—in knowledge and communications skills—depends upon the care and detail we put into the questions we ask and the degree to which we actively listen.

Today he might use as an example Colonel Peck, the Marine Corps officer who testified to a congressional committee in regards to allowing homosexuals into the military. What, he might ask, should students think when they hear Colonel Peck saying he would fear for his own homosexual son's life should his son, Scott, decide to join the military. What flaw in Marine Corps training, Spencer might ask, and "what weakness in their discipline would lead Marines to attack—brutally, perhaps fatally—a colleague whose sexual orientation is different from their own?" (Raspberry, 1993, May 19, p. 11A). And what flaw in human education in general would allow this issue to remain unaddressed for all those pre–Marine Corps years?

Are Americans today learning what is best for the individual *and* what is necessary for our country to become a better place for everyone? Are the public spaces we share becoming a beacon for people from all walks of life? Is common goodness increasing? Is America becoming a safer place to raise our children?

We smile at the supermarket headlines of the *Sun, Globe, Star,* and *National Examiner* and perhaps even chuckle aloud at the *Weekly World News,* but the headlines of the *Chicago Tribune, Los Angeles Times,* or *Boston Globe* cause little amusement: "Boys Use Gun to Rob Girl, 9" (*The Free Press,* March 2, 1988); "Actress Slashed by Gang on N.Y. Street" (*Minneapolis Star Tribune,* January 14, 1990); "Violence Erupts at Dallas Cowboys' Super Bowl Rally" (*Saint Paul Pioneer Press,* February 10, 1993). Americans are no longer shocked and are far from outraged. They are simply numb to hatred, crime, and violence.

These are the realities today: children who cannot sleep near windows for fear of being struck by a stray bullet; retired people unable to go out at night to play pinochle; citizens afraid to document unlawful behavior. In small midwestern communities, automobile windows are damaged by pellet guns or .22 rifles, rocks are thrown from interstate overpasses onto traffic below, and snow blowers, even while being used, are stolen at gun point ("Car windows shot," 1993; Wangstad, 1994; "Teens dropping rocks," 1991; "Two charged in," 1993).

Perhaps President Clinton is right when he says, "Unless we do something about the crime and drugs and violence that is ravaging our country, it will destroy us" ("Clinton: A 'crisis,' " 1993, p. 16A).

WHAT AMERICANS NEED TO LEARN

America does have problems, and our curriculum should reflect a concern for them. It should also reflect an attempt to resolve them. We believe schools should help citizens learn the following:

• Before graduation, schools should require each student to demonstrate an understanding of pluralism and its main root, the principle of individual human dignity.

They should require students to know that different groups (e.g., a religious sect, a black organization, a woman's liberation group, or a sportsman's club) "have the right to exist, protected from intrusion or domination by outsiders considered to have alien values" (Unruh & Unruh, 1984), p. 114).

And schools should require students to demonstrate that they *can* see people as individuals and can judge them according to their ability, character, intelligence, and talent—not their race, age, sexual orientation, religious dispositions, financial assets, or family structure.

• Students need to know that "on a wide range of matters, there is no fixed, let alone official, black position" (Hacker, 1992, p. 43), and that it is silly for white persons to ask minority persons to tell them how "their group" thinks about some individual or issue.

No one would desire to be held responsible for what every person of his or her color thinks or does. Blacks, for example, do not need to atone for some utterances of Louis Farrakhan or Khalid Abdul Muhammad or assert that they do not speak for them, nor do they need to justify or condemn the "black hustlers who manipulate white guilt and white fear to their own self advantage" (Harrington, 1992, p. 307). Minorities would like to live their lives, not explain their lives. None of us wants to get bogged down by how we perceive other people perceiving us. Like all Americans, minorities are quite capable of choosing their own causes and have no obligation to follow agendas set by others (Hacker, 1992). Students need to know such things.

• Students should graduate knowing there are no easy solutions to major problems. For example, in the area of handgun control and waiting periods, students need to know that "gangbangers" and drug dealers "aren't deterred by registration or cooling off laws. They don't shop at sporting marts with the skeet-shooting crowd. Their gun suppliers deal out of car trunks or abandoned buildings" (Royko, 1993, p. 5).

• Students need to demonstrate they know teenagers don't deliberately get pregnant to go on welfare. Instead, "they have babies to increase their self-esteem, to give themselves 'something to love' in a world where delayed gratification seems pointless" (Kaus, 1992, p. 177).

• Prior to graduation students need to know colleges and universities have a vocational function. They need to understand that it is academic snobbery to talk about "mere jobs" versus "professions." They need to respect jobs requiring verbal skill and abstract reasoning as well as jobs requiring craftsmanship.

• Before graduation students need to demonstrate they understand the role of mass media. That is, they need to know that the goal of most television is to keep them entertained, so when the real message—the commercial—comes along, they will still be available. They need to realize whatever will pass censors and keep buyers glued to the television set will be provided. They also need to know that invasive commercialism "has damaged everyone by ceaselessly claiming that the road to happiness is a new Volvo or tennis shoes or an eight-ball jacket" (Harrington, 1992, p. 364).

But because television is so much a part of everyone's life, students also need to know there are some reasonably good television networks (e.g., CNN, PBS, C-Span, Discovery) and on nearly every channel some worthwhile programs. Students need exposure to a variety of programs for all the obvious reasons, but also so they'll be less likely to become what rapper Father MC says they already are: "bored with everything but sex and money" (Marriott, 1993).

Students need to know that what is seen on television is often a distortion of reality. What they see is a writer's, director's, and producer's sense of reality. Unfortunately, this is even true of the news. (In 1968, during the takeover of Columbia University, one of the authors saw a camera operator move from behind the camera and direct persons as to how they should hold their protest signs and what they should say. That evening this "program," as directed, was shown on *national* television.) Every school should create a course that focuses upon how easily a camera and the director can distort reality. We should teach students to become less tolerant of those who wish to manipulate us.

• Students need to know that brutality and lawlessness in America are not new and that "we have always been a violent society" (Flanery, 1993, p. 1). Communities that sprang up during the gold and silver discoveries, cow towns at the end of cattle trails, river villages with saw mills, water stops and switching yards on the rail lines, and so on, were known for their bullies and those who lacked respect for imposed rules.

From 1889 to 1940 there were 3,833 persons lynched (Myrdal, 1944); and during World War II, hoodlums beat up older Jewish persons, desecrated Jewish cemeteries, defiled synagogues, and terrorized local newsstand proprietors and movie patrons (Tenenbaum, 1947). What is different about today is the dramatic expansion of personal mobility and the degree of individual freedom from the family, the village, and the law. People who "kept their noses clean" and avoided "certain" areas were at one time secure. This is no longer true. We are all vulnerable to predatory behavior at any time, anywhere. By knowing this, students will hopefully become more inclined to be supportive of, and empathetic toward, those who have been violated.

- Students need to be aware that words can hurt as much as sticks and stones. They need to graduate knowing some mean-spirited behaviors go far beyond the teenagers' prank. They need to graduate knowing that those tormented never forget their tormentors (Greene, 1993, April 29).

- Students need to know that less than one generation ago motel clerks commonly "lost" minority guests' reservations once they saw them in person; marriage between blacks and whites (miscegenation) was illegal, a felony, in sixteen states (Oppenheimer, 1993); and "stores wouldn't sell a black woman a dress if some white woman had already bought that one" (Harrington, 1992, p. 221).

Students need to know that many blacks living today have for at least part of their lives been obliged for protracted periods of time to look for places to relieve themselves, get a drink, or get a sandwich. Whites need to know how very much they are asking blacks to put behind them when they say, "trust me, I am different" (Harrington, 1992).

- Before graduation students need to understand that they live in a country that claims it cannot afford to underwrite more summer jobs, and cannot afford more Head Start teachers, and cannot afford more staffing for afterschool and summer recreational facilities, and more elementary guidance counselors, and more drama directors so every student who wants to can be in a play, yet *each year* it spends $5.6 billion for cookies, $8 billion for pornography, $62 billion for toilet articles, barber shops, hair salons and other cosmetic indulgences, and $18.8 billion for lottery tickets (Goldstein, 1993).

- Students need to know that rape is not about sex but about power and control. They need to know that rape is an ugly act of dominance and that sex is simply used as a weapon "to humiliate, embarrass, and degrade the victim" (Dowd, 1993, p. 5).

Rapists cannot carry out their acts unless they are prepared to beat their victims into submission or threaten them with injury or death. Even if victims submit, they may still be maimed or killed, since sexual conquest does not always satiate the rapist (Hacker, 1992). "A rapist is a single-minded, totally self-absorbed, sociopathic beast—a beast that cannot be tamed with understanding" (Vachss, 1993, p. 6).

- Students need to learn that "it is hard to be a member of any minority—whether it be a minority in beliefs, dress, customs, color—or in any way" (Tenenbaum, 1947, p. 84).

- Before graduation students need to demonstrate they understand stereotypes, arrogance, generalizations about an entire group, and the "imposition of majority cultural standards of thinking and behavior on those" who are not like themselves (Jones, 1993, p. 23A). When a white person "compliments" a black person by saying, "I don't see you as a black person" or "I don't consider you black," the white is *not* demonstrating acceptance. He or she is not giving a compliment. Such statements simply confirm what every black American knows: that America "is a white country which expects its inhabitants to think and act in white ways" (Hacker, 1992, p. 33).

"All blacks are unfairly stigmatized by the behavior of the underclass minority" (Kaus, 1992, p. 106), and students need to *feel* this before they graduate. They need to know that "most poor people of all races labor honestly, even for a small return. By the same token, persons who do choose to break the law come from every tier in the social structure" (Hacker, 1992, p. 184).

• Students need to understand *why* many people of color are not "overly grateful" or "sufficiently humble" when white people point out to them how life for minorities in America is better than it used to be.

Why should they be grateful? Most of their great-great-great-grandparents were born in America. The United States *is* their home. Doors should never have been shut to them because of their color in the first place. Things may be 100 times better for minorities today than in the past, but by any standard minorities are still far from equal with the majority population. "If someone is beating you three times a day and switched to twice a day, is life better?" (Harrington, 1992, p. 272).

• Students need to know that when they hear people saying that blacks or Latinos are hard to work with ("We had one but he didn't work out."), or that blacks or Latinos have a chip on their shoulders, or that blacks are unable to relax in workplace relationships, they need to ask why. If indeed many members of minorities do act in these ways, why?

We have all had our behaviors misinterpreted by coworkers and those with authority. Wouldn't it be nice to have one of them, who cares, ask *why* we feel as we do?

• Students need to know that when a white watches the tape of Rodney King getting beaten, he or she might say something like, "Look what they're doing to that poor guy!" But when a black male watches that tape, he would be almost sure to say, "My God! That could be me" (Church, 1992, p. 20).

Students need to know that the African-American community wants strong, tough, honest, fair policing, and that there is no African-American community in the United States that does not want to see police there. The African-American community just wants to be treated fairly. African-Americans just want to be treated honestly and with dignity (Levy, 1992). They simply want those who enforce the law to be able to distinguish between law-abiding citizens and local predators, and they want the police to "use force that is reasonable and necessary—and no more" (Mathews, 1993, p. 21).

It is much like the uproar surrounding whether to teach *Huckleberry Finn*. Black people just want *Huckleberry Finn* taught by a teacher who understands that the word *nigger* hurts and is "associated with slavery and beating and lynching and deprivations of all sorts" ("Racial slurs may," 1994, p. 3B). They just want it taught by a teacher who can put into perspective, for white teenagers, Mark Twain's intentions when he used the term.

• Students need to know that many blacks do not spout the white liberalisms about how society is to blame for black poverty and despair. They believe it but reject it at once because they know it's no use telling a young man he's a victim of his environment. They know he can't call his daddy's friends for a job. They know "he's gotta get up and do it, carry the extra weight, or sink" (Harrington, 1992, p. 334).

• Whites need to know that blacks *aren't* just like them. Blacks and whites are the same *and* different. How could blacks and whites not be different? They "have literally lived in a different land and country for four hundred years" (Harrington, 1992, p. 446).

• Students need to know that many blacks are offended by the question: "Is it better or worse for blacks today?" because that question "carries an implicit question whites won't ask: If it's better why are you still complaining?" (Harrington, 1992, p. 272). Racism is still pervasive in America, and we cannot stop talking about it or people will forget it.

• Before graduation students need to demonstrate an understanding of the fourth R, respect: respect for neighbors, for differences, and especially respect for themselves. They also need to demonstrate an understanding of the causes of self-destructive behavior, underachievement, and self-pity.

SUMMARY

This is by no means a complete list of what we believe students should learn before graduation, but it does contain a sample. After reading it you may be thinking, "Good list—I'll try teaching these things," or you may be thinking, "Well, I'm already doing this," or you may simply be thinking of that cynical but wise old man, Thomas Hobbes, "who proved rather conclusively that, while any person's actual possibilities to improve the lot of his fellow creatures amounted to almost nothing, everyone's opportunity to do damage was always immense. The wisest and most virtuous man will hardly leave a print in the sand behind him, meant Hobbes, but an imbecile crank can set fire to a whole town" (Myrdal, 1944, p. 79).

The key, it seems, is the teacher's ability to generate a positive attitude and to get students to face reality without giving up hope—these are the fine lines that teachers must walk.

The Hidden Curriculum: What We Unintentionally Teach and Learn

It's very feasible, Space Marketing CEO Mike Lawson said Tuesday. We could actually fly (a corporate logo such as McDonald's) "Golden Arches" in space and it might appear as large as the full moon.

Space Marketing hopes to launch the first space billboard in 1996.

The orbital advertising sign is being produced in collaboration with engineers at Lawrence Livermore National Laboratory and the University of Colorado. ("Firm wants to," 1993, p. 12)

Unanticipated collateral learnings are as significant as the targeted material. Chapter 3 focuses upon this issue.

What we unintentionally teach is often as important as what we teach through our designed curricula. Making an assignment requiring a father's participation when a child has no resident father "teaches" what we do not intend. Lecturing with little input from students sends a message different from that sent by using the discussion method. And listening in a nonjudgmental manner speaks volumes.

CURRICULUM DEFINED

The term *curriculum* is one most people understand. If the public school has just "updated its curriculum" or if "liberals have joined conservatives in attacking the heavily 'politically correct' content of the curriculum," most of us know what is being talked about. It is a term like *discipline*. If you say, "the discipline in our school is getting lax!" most of us understand.

When people use the term *curriculum*, they generally mean the content pupils are expected to learn or the subjects offered for study at school. Curriculum writers, of course, define it in quite specific ways. Franklin Bobbitt (1918), for example, says it is a "series of experiences which children and youth must have by way of attaining . . . objectives" (p. 42). Daniel Tanner and Laurel Tanner (1980), on the other hand, regard curriculum as "that reconstruction of knowledge and experience, systematically developed under the auspices of the school (or university), to enable the learner to increase his or her control of knowledge and experience" (p. 43). As you can see, curriculum writers take their definitions quite seriously.

Some curriculum specialists see the term as specific (the courses taught) and others—for example, Giroux, Penna, and Pinar (1981)—see it as broad (everything that transpires in the course of planning, teaching, and learning in an educational institution).

Those who see the term as narrow agree that we have two curricula in our schools: the *formal curriculum*, the one nearly all think about when they use the term, and the *hidden curriculum*, the curriculum most do not realize exists.

FORMAL CURRICULUM

The formal curriculum is the planned, acknowledged, official curriculum—the curriculum that spells out the content to be covered and the courses to be taught, the curriculum over which students are tested, the document citizens view to determine what K–12 students learn and when they learn it. This formal curriculum is the one that includes the knowledge that teachers, curriculum developers, administrators, State Department of Education members, Board of Teaching members, legislators, and selected groups of parents believe is worthy of inclusion within a formal course of study. It is the content (reading, writing, arithmetic, history, etc.) that is generally neither controversial nor sensitive.

HIDDEN CURRICULUM

The hidden curriculum is the other curriculum in our schools. It contains the collateral learnings students acquire—the enduring attitudes they develop toward what is learned and toward learning itself. It is the unplanned, informal, unacknowledged curriculum. It includes things taught that are not in daily lesson plans and involves content not reviewed before exams. It includes feelings a person remembers from an experience.

Impact of the Hidden Curriculum

The impact of the hidden curriculum can be positive or negative. Students can learn positive attitudes, appreciations, values, and behaviors from their environment, classmates, and teachers, or students can learn enduring negative dispositions of thought from the hidden curriculum, such as after graduation never wanting to set foot in a classroom again.

If a school has positive, uplifting banners in the hallways and attractive items in display cases, a message is sent.

If middle school or junior high students are allowed to have dances during school hours, a message is sent.

If parents are invited to a school breakfast honoring their child, a message is sent.

If students are allowed to wear tee shirts advertising beer or containing swear words, a message is sent.

If interracial dating is banned, a message is sent ("Principal suspended in," 1994).

If the school allows students to eat breakfast before school begins, if the principal hires friendly secretaries (who make students and guests feel welcome), if cooks and custodians are considerate, messages are sent.

If a school sets aside one-half hour each week for *everyone* to read, a message is sent.

What is read on the intercom, and what appears in the announcements, sends a message.

The hidden curriculum is taught in the hallways, in the cafeteria, in the main office, *and* in the classroom.

Hidden Curriculum in the Classroom

Every teacher at every grade level teaches a hidden curriculum. How teachers' rooms are arranged, the rules they post, the bulletin boards they display, the students' work they place on the walls, what they use for a bathroom pass, whether file cabinets are locked—all these visual things, and hundreds more, teach the hidden curriculum. These nonverbal messages are powerful because the nonverbal always communicates more clearly, effectively, and purely than does the verbal.

The hidden curriculum includes those things we teach without making a special point to do so and includes how we teach. The *process* is as important as the *content*. The way we teach is as important as what we teach. For example, if a minority view is shouted down and not intelligently discussed, a definite attitude or disposition is learned by everyone in the classroom.

The hidden curriculum includes how late papers and students who are late to class are handled, how wrong answers are responded to, how much quiet is expected during videotapes and films, and how much "busy work" is assigned.

If students pass history but hate history, if students learn that only the biggest and meanest get their way, if students learn that it is okay not to try in school, what is the gain?

The hidden curriculum includes the way teachers conduct themselves around students and how they allow students to behave around each other.

Making positive use of the hidden curriculum can be as simple as smiling or just listening or making an encouraging gesture or explaining why a particular unit is being studied, or even establishing eye contact. It can be simple, but can also be powerful. The hidden curriculum has at least as much to do with the formation of morals, values, and personal ethics as does the formal curriculum.

Hidden Curriculum from a Broader Perspective

Generally we associate the term *curriculum* with schooling, but the truth is we are surrounded by a curriculum: The content of movies, the tabloid headlines at checkout lanes, the content of regular network and cable television, the way the "good old boys" at work treat us, the columnists an editor allows in his or her local newspaper, these are all curricula. We are surrounded by voices willing and eager to tell us what to believe and what will, if we purchase it, make us happy. It takes deliberate effort every day, nearly every minute, to live as *we* believe life should be lived.

Bookstores that encourage browsing, coffee houses that foster quiet conversations, theaters having zero tolerance policies toward disrespectful behaviors, and museums that discourage unattended children still exist. And if one goes at the right time, during the right season, he or she can still enjoy a quiet, reflective walk in the park.

It is, of course, becoming more difficult to control the curriculum we are exposed to. But to a degree it can be done. One of the authors, for example, rarely watches television news, reads four or five newspapers each day to access a variety of columnists, and watches only television programs that have been taped so commercials can be fast-forwarded and therefore avoided.

Avoiding the curriculum being pounded into us also requires a little luck. For example, by getting to the San Jacinto Monument and Museum of History, or to the tomb of Abraham Lincoln, or to the National Civil Rights Museum well before a tour bus of loud, disrespectful people arrives or after a busload of uncontrolled school children leaves, one can still enjoy the curriculum offered by these magnificent places.

SUMMARY

We are surrounded by curricula. We are asked to learn nearly every waking hour. Often, however, it is those with wealth and power and a concern for only more of the same who do the teaching. We must become keenly aware of this and do what we can to reduce their influence.

Teachers must also start considering the hidden curriculum in our schools with the same seriousness they consider the written, formal curriculum (Ryan, 1993).

4

An Untapped Source of Hope: Elementary and Secondary Teachers Mentoring One Another

> Our age is not the first to have reaped the ruin resulting from an enlargement of men's [or women's] powers, unaccompanied by growth in the capacity to control them. (Tawney, 1931, p. 189)

If elementary and secondary teachers take a graduate class together, work closely, and talk openly, what do they come to believe about each other?

Do secondary teachers leave the class believing elementary teachers are narrow-minded, petty, picky, and possessive? Do they leave thinking elementary teachers have fewer and less severe problems?

What, on the other hand, do elementary teachers leave believing about secondary teachers? Do they see them as being less caring, dedicated, and concerned about the whole child? Do they come away from the class believing secondary teachers are arrogant?

We wanted to be able to answer such questions, so for the past ten years when teaching graduate classes attended by nearly equal numbers of veteran secondary and elementary teachers, we asked these questions: What insights have you gained and what have you concluded about secondary (elementary) teachers? Does a gap exist between the two groups? Please elaborate.

From their responses, our conversations with them, and observations of their interactions, we conclude the following:

When elementary and secondary teachers work together for an extended period, in formal settings, *secondary teachers come to believe that elementary teachers*

- have too little time to prepare lesson plans
- have too many demands placed upon them
- have class sizes far too large
- should have no class larger than twenty students
- should be praised for being able to exhibit tolerance and patience when working with the same group of children for an entire day
- give too much praise
- do too much to cushion future consequences of student misbehavior
- are more perceptive in seeing student problems (possibly because secondary students are better at disguising personal problems)
- fear some students
- do not let students make enough mistakes (thus depriving them of a most effective way to learn)
- waste time making bulletin boards when students could do it better and learn in the process
- are more united among themselves than secondary teachers

When elementary and secondary teachers work together for an extended period, in formal settings, *elementary teachers come to believe that secondary teachers*

- work with too many students each day
- are intimidated (usually the men) by younger children
- too seldom share their positive feelings toward students
- too infrequently recognize birthdays and place outstanding work on classroom walls
- give too much superficial praise
- do not use (or carelessly use) bulletin boards as learning tools
- do not appreciate the fact that eleventh-graders seldom wet their pants during class
- are more united than elementary teachers

When elementary and secondary teachers work together for an extended period in professional settings, *they come to agree that*

- every teacher, even the best, has problems
- every student, regardless of grade level, has many of the same basic needs
- teaching is a team effort with all parties, at all grade levels, needed to complete a student's education
- individual students' personalities do not change drastically from grade school to high school

- no age group is necessarily "worse" or "harder to handle" than any other
- all students need guidance, leadership, and support
- at times, administrators are difficult persons with whom to deal
- every teacher, deep in his or her heart, wishes to produce responsible, literate, human beings
- a good teacher is a good listener
- classroom rules should be basically the same K–12
- students are starved for attention
- there is too little interaction between elementary and secondary teachers
- teachers who care and show respect for students are respected by parents, colleagues, administrators, and students at every grade level
- children at every grade level need to know where they stand and what is expected
- reasons behind misbehavior are similar regardless of age level

From working with graduate students for many years and from working with elementary and secondary cooperating teachers on a daily basis, we have come to believe that elementary and secondary teachers are much more similar than different, much more tolerant and accepting of one another than old stereotypes would suggest, and more supportive of one another's efforts than many may believe.

REPRESENTATIVE SAMPLES OF WHAT HUNDREDS OF TEACHERS WROTE

"I think the elementary and secondary gap has a lot to do with the idea that each does not understand the problems they both face. I feel they should get together a lot more and talk with each other and share their ideas and problems."

"As a secondary teacher I sometimes forget that elementary teachers have the same discipline problems. I do think elementary teachers are more creative in their approach and often times are willing to show more caring. As a secondary teacher I am really going to try to show my love and care to each student."

"It is most obvious from our class that secondary and elementary teachers learn from each other. At least I feel this way. It might be just to realize that even though we are with different grade levels, we have the same frustrations."

"The class made me realize that the discipline problems primary people have are basically similar to the ones secondary teachers have—they just vary in the degree and in the punishment."

"I have come to believe that the roles we play are much more similar than what I thought as a young teacher. We have come to compartmentalize our roles as education has become more 'sophisticated,' and this is unfortunate."

"It seems behavior problems become compounded as the child gets older. The reasons most likely remain the same, but the acting out becomes more violent in the secondary schools. By watching and listening to secondary teachers relate their discipline problems, I can reflect on the importance of going after the reason for the misbehavior when I have them in first grade. By helping to take care of the reason early in school, these children wouldn't be a problem later and hence would be more successful."

SUMMARY AND RECOMMENDATIONS

We believe that schooling at the elementary and secondary levels is intended to do two things: (1) to help students make sense of their world and (2) to provide understandings necessary for functioning and surviving in today's society. We further believe that to achieve these ends teachers must teach students how to reason, how to think critically, and how to communicate with those who are different from themselves.

All day, while working with children that come to school with problems most Americans could not even imagine, teachers are expected to be sensitive and tolerant. They are expected to give of themselves, to be supportive, to listen, to resolve conflicts, to provide praise.

But who helps teachers? Where and when can they appear vulnerable and unknowledgeable? Who listens to their concerns, encourages their idealism, helps them maintain their self-respect? Who gives them strokes and fills their "confidence bucket"? Who helps them to recognize their blind spots? A principal's shoulders cannot be this broad.

Partial solutions, however, can be as near as the next school building. We believe that when given a chance to work together, elementary and secondary teachers quickly learn to accept, support, and respect one another.

Administrators, we believe, would be wise to create opportunities in professional settings for elementary and secondary teachers to work together on common concerns. This, in our opinion, is one of the greatest untapped resources we have for faculty renewal. It is one of the best opportunities available for teachers to reinforce each other's needs to dream and to recapture their idealism.

Teachers *need* to view teaching from a different perspective; "they need to explore the thinking behind their practices" (Garmston, Lindner, & Whitaker, 1993, p. 57); they need to ask anew what business they are in, decide upon new missions, and remind themselves of why they became teachers in the first place. Such interactions release a positive energy and create a hope-filled environment. These interactions reinforce the positive and allow teachers to become America's best hope for survival.

5

Socially Inconsiderate People

As long as women admire tough, macho men who are always ready for a fight, men will be encouraged to behave that way. (Meier, 1993, p. 3E)

Several years ago, Katharine Hepburn stopped mid-sentence during the Broadway play "The West Side Waltz" and said to a patron, "You must take your feet off the stage." Later, during curtain call, the same patron, in violation of a long-established Broadway policy, photographed her using a flash camera. This time Hepburn exploded. "You must never again do a thing like that in the theater!" Then remembering his feet on the stage, she added, "I was expecting that the next thing you'd want was for me to bring you a pipe and slippers. You shouldn't be a boor. You shouldn't pick on us like that, being rude, because we are sitting ducks up here."

Would an actress today lecture an audience on "concert etiquette"? Or have members of our contemporary society become "afraid to tell anyone that anything is wrong and off limits" (Greene, 1993, February 11, p. 5)?

Can socially inconsiderate behaviors that diminish everyone's enjoyment of public spaces be reduced—reduced, that is, *without* the majority, in a fit of self-righteousness, ravishing the minority? (e.g., when a schizophrenic stabs to death a pregnant mother of three, can an enraged society be kept from "dismissing the needs of thousands of others [schizophrenics] who are no threat to the community what-so-ever" ("Diana pleads for," 1993, p. 2)?

Chapter 5 addresses the issue of social inconsiderateness. It considers a number of questions: Who are these socially inconsiderate persons? Should we react to socially inconsiderate behavior? How might we feel if we choose not to confront socially inconsiderate behavior? What do we need to keep in mind if we choose to confront socially inconsiderate people? What can educators do to make our society more kind, gentle, and humane?

We realize, of course, that some readers may find such a chapter, with its concern for "Victorian-era politeness," petty and whiny, especially in light of the world's enormous problems (e.g., extermination squads killing thousands of poor street children in Brazil's cities each year, "robber-barons" plundering people's life savings, and environmental catastrophes around every corner) ("8 children killed," 1993). But we include it because educators *can* ease societal concerns about socially inconsiderate behavior; they can arrest this "New York attitude that is taking over the whole country" (Carroll, 1992, p. 3E); and they can help America become a more pleasant, civil, and enjoyable place for everyone.

WHO ARE THESE SOCIALLY INCONSIDERATE PERSONS?

Socially inconsiderate persons are those who annoy us. They are people who exhibit behaviors that can, in spite of ourselves, cause us to feel anxious, disgusted, and deeply upset. They are those who

- act as if they are better than people who don't or didn't go to college
- pull out in front of us in their car, as if in a hurry, and then poke along
- refuse to smile or say hello
- do not signal before they turn
- deliberately use more than one parking space so no one will nick their precious car
- roll down their car window and throw out trash
- tell a one-minute story in fifteen minutes
- let their children get away with tantrums in grocery stores

Socially inconsiderate people are the ones Mike Royko, the columnist from Chicago, frequently writes about, the ones even his positive and optimistic readers make time to criticize. They are, for example, drivers who slow down and speed up, drive on the shoulder, then on the center line, because they are preoccupied while talking on their cellular telephones.

Socially inconsiderate people are those who never ask how you are or how your work is going. They are the ones who never say, "It's on me," or ask, "What's your opinion?" or "Is there anything I can do to help?" (Rose, 1993). They are the ones who "badger another person with sexual come-ons when the attention is unwelcomed" ("Sexual harassment picture," 1993, p. 24).

They are the people who carry their portable telephones into the movie theaters, and when they ring during the movie answer with "Oh, hi! How are you?" and then carry on a five-minute conversation "in a regular tone of voice as if it was the most natural thing in the world to be doing" (Greene, 1993, March 16, p. 5). They are the ones at the fast food restaurant who shove each other and throw food at each other and make a mess on the table and floor and carry on a loud and profane conversation that disturbs everyone (Geewax, 1993, December). They are the people who say by their behavior, "I'm more important than you. I'm sufficiently important to intrude my personal space on yours" (Carroll, 1992, June 30, p. 3E). Socially inconsiderate people, of which our country has an abundance, are those who make life in America *less* pleasant for everyone.

REACTING TO SOCIALLY INCONSIDERATE BEHAVIOR

How reluctant is our society to pass judgment?

How do you react to store clerks who ignore you and continue to chat among themselves? Those who drive without a muffler? Those who cut in line when patrons are queued up at the movie house? Those who talk loudly in the library? Protesting zealots who forget good manners and politeness and attempt to bully? The removal of pay telephones from neighhborhoods where the inhabitants can least afford them in their home, taken out because gang members use the booths as their offices (Greene, 1992, September 8)?

Ellen Goodman (1993) asserts that our society has undergone a moral lobotomy, and she asks: "In the reluctance, the aversion—dare I say phobia—to being judgmental, are we disabled from making any judgments at all" (p. 4)?

Should we react to socially inconsiderate behavior? Or by confronting people are we needlessly going out on a limb and begging trouble? After all, many of those who shake their fists at us when we do not move quickly enough at the stop light or threaten to bash our brains out if we attempt to take "their" parking space may well be persons who until very recently were confined to mental hospitals, or they may be one of those 3 million people on our streets who have just been released from jail or prison, are on parole, or are awaiting a hearing or trial (Anderson et al., 1992).

We may not wish to react physically to every socially inconsiderate behavior because in America some people like Steve Palermo and Chris Petteroff, people with real names who live in real communities, do get shot or stabbed when they confront those unaccustomed to having limits placed upon their actions ("Palermo surgery encouraging," 1993; "Man stabbed while," 1993).

HOW SHOULD WE FEEL IF WE CHOOSE NOT TO
CONFRONT SOCIALLY INCONSIDERATE PEOPLE?

Should we feel like cowards? Should our dates still respect us if we let people berate us and do nothing?

Let's return for a moment to Ms. Hepburn and "The West Side Waltz" and the audience's reaction to her explosion. A newspaper account of the Hepburn incident read, "The audience broke into cheers at her rebuke, and the man faded into the crowd as the theater emptied" (Hepburn scolds 'boor,' " 1982, p. 14).

It would be nice, of course, to receive the psychological and physical support Ms. Hepburn received when she scolded the boor, but the reality is we will often feel very much alone. In fact, it may be necessary for us at times to flee or to lie and tell a person he or she is right even though he or she is most definitely in error. This is *not* cowardly behavior, nor should we feel that it is.

It may also become necessary, at extreme moments, to get down on our knees and beg. Again, in spite of how Randolph Scott, of western movie fame, and Jim Rockford, of "the Rockford Files," have taught us to behave, this may *not* be cowardly behavior. It may simply be an intelligent and a healthy response to what each of us may one day encounter.

Our society includes thousands who act out any urge that pops into their heads. We are all vulnerable—more so than anyone of us would ever like to believe. We must never allow those who do not value their own lives, those who may not even remember the encounter the next day, to make us feel guilty for doing what will keep us alive.

WHAT TO KEEP IN MIND SHOULD WE CHOOSE TO
REACT TO SOCIALLY INCONSIDERATE BEHAVIOR

In spite of the strange and unjust behaviors going on all around us, we need to keep in mind that most people behave rudely out of ignorance, by accident, or because they cannot behave any differently, not because they believe the bold, vocal, and aggressive are the only people with rights.

It is very difficult to believe this, we know, but *most* people, at least 90 percent of them, when not on drugs are reasonable and fair. Even people identified as relentlessly rude take advantage of graceful retreats if offered (Martin, 1991). We need to believe that rudeness may be accidental. By believing this we can react in ways that provide the offender a face-saving escape. Making statements such as "Excuse me but I believe I was here first" or "I don't believe that's permitted here" will work if the tone in our voice, the gestures we exhibit, and the expressions upon our face give every clue and hint that we genuinely believe the offender's behavior was accidental or engaged in out of ignorance.

WHAT EDUCATORS CAN DO TO MAKE OUR SOCIETY MORE KIND, GENTLE, AND HUMANE

Educators can do more than give lip-service to the ideal of making our pluralistic and democratic society more kind, gentle, and humane. They can achieve these ends by supporting those who have been treated rudely, by comforting those who have experienced uncivilized behaviors, by giving a positive gesture or a supportive word to those "decents" who try to do the right thing, and by modeling behaviors that show respect for the dignity of every person.

We will never totally prevent the extreme cases of unacceptable conduct such as the muggings and assaults that took place after the Human Kindness Day held in Washington, D.C., in 1975; or the purse grabbings and the slashings that occurred after the 1983 Diana Ross concert in Central Park. Nor will we ever totally prevent the inaction of spectators, such as in the Kitty Genovese case of 1967, where the Queens, New York, woman was fatally stabbed on an ordinary street as ordinary people watched from apartment windows and listened to her screams; or the incident in St. Louis in 1983 where a thirteen-year-old girl was raped for forty minutes by two youths as several people stood by. (Incidentally, police in the St. Louis incident were finally summoned by an eleven-year-old boy.) But we can teach that no one ever deserves to be raped or to have rings ripped from fingers.

We can teach that the ancient practice of exercising random acts of human kindness (Salter, 1993) should be renewed because such acts make life more pleasant for all. We can also teach that "when you turn your back on your neighbor's attack by hoodlums, you have lessened your own safety and increased the likelihood of your own home being attacked by hoodlums" (Tenenbaum, 1947, p. 157).

SUMMARY

Although the socially inconsiderate behaviors of playing a radio loudly on a public bus, of engaging in sex under a blanket at a public park, and of putting one's feet upon a stage during a theater performance are a far cry from the cases cited above, which occurred in New York, Washington, D.C., and St. Louis, they are nonetheless behaviors that make life less pleasant.

Some rude and boorish behavior will always be with us unfortunately, yet we should never be reluctant to summon authorities. Nor should we, when prudent, be reluctant to confront unacceptable behaviors because left unchecked, they can only escalate. The price we pay for living in a free society must never be the toleration of behavior that takes emotional warmth from our souls or laughter and carefreeness from our lives (Myrdal, Sterner, & Rose, 1944).

Part Two

Attitudes toward and Perceptions of Greed, Ethics, Morals, Values, and Indifference

6

Greed

Greed is a bottomless pit which exhausts the person in an endless effort to satisfy the need without ever reaching satisfaction. (Fromm, 1965, p. 136)

Greed, the excessive desire for money, position, or possessions such as land, works of art, or jewels, conjures up images of selfishness, indifference to suffering, accumulation far exceeding need, and lust for power. It can be a tool to achieve fame, a weapon to gain financial advantage, or a scourge to punish. The greedy never have enough, are never satisfied.

Chapter 6 investigates the role of greed and its effect upon society, ethics, morals, and values.

GREED AND SOCIETY

When looking for reasons why a society fails, one usually finds basic greed at the root of its demise. When a society allows greed, selfishness, and indifference to take precedence over rules of conduct, laws that govern, and working for mutual benefit and the common good, it becomes a society in imminent danger of failure.

If permitted to expand unchecked, greed has deleterious effects on all. It endangers the ethics, morals, and positive values held by members of a society. Without rules or laws, a society begins to degenerate. Eventually it is taken over by another society or putrefies from within and disintegrates. That is the lesson to be learned from history.

Greed occurs when a society loses its focus upon the great ideals and concerns that were the original rationale for its formation. It occurs when selfishness and self-centeredness prevail over the rights of individuals and when self-importance becomes paramount.

Greed makes people question the rules or codes of behavior that were passed onto them. It can even cause people to make unethical decisions, ones that if reconsidered would not ordinarily be made. Greed eats away at resistance and resolution at moments of personal weakness, at moments when alcohol or drugs cloud the mind. Such eroding of one's conscience and resistance may occur during periods of anger, resentment, jealousy, or fear, times when ethical and moral beliefs can be more easily momentarily rejected.

Greed affects the individual and the society but also manifests itself at the national and international levels. Camouflaged by its use as a "bargaining chip" in which one nation withholds goods and services to gain political advantage over another, greed can result in nations literally being held hostage.

A current and continuing example is the destruction of the rain forests in South America, Indonesia, and Africa. The countries as well as foreign investors involved insist that lumber is needed for export, more land is needed for crops, and more jobs are needed for domestic labor; and nations which have already depleted their resources need the raw materials. Some nations, however, are concerned that uncontrolled deforestation will contribute to global warming, to a loss of oxygen-producing plants, to the annihilation of plant and animal species (many of which have not yet been classified, many with potential medical benefits), and to the pollution of streams, rivers, and oceans. The result is finger-pointing. Who are the greedy nations, and where should the blame lie?

Another area of international concern is that of the indiscriminate use of chemicals for insect and weed control. A classic example is DDT (dichloro-diphenial-triethane). In her book *Silent Spring*, Rachael Carson (1962) made people aware of the deleterious effects of DDT to both humans and animals, especially birds. DDT is no longer used in the United States, but it is manufactured in Third World nations, where it currently is being used as a cheap insecticide.

Countries compete with each other to gain more market share for manufactured goods, stockpile mineral resources, and use political influence to gain access to renewable commodities such as timber and nonrenewal commodities such as oil and natural gas, as well as other raw materials. They seek access to icefree ports or ocean ports, trade status, and taxation advantage. Is this greed or need?

All of us are susceptible to greed, but greed affects some more than others. It affects individuals, states, even countries. We seldom call greed for what it is, but nevertheless the characteristics are all there. One example of this is water rights. Who owns water? The first person upstream? The country where the water source begins? Who has the right to unlimited use? Courts are currently deciding the answers to these questions at international, federal, state, and local levels. Another example is that of a company or corporation that sinks wells deeper than most and lowers the water level to the point where individual wells no longer produce.

States compete with each other to see which can receive the most federal aid, industrial plants, and disaster assistance. Each seeks as much as possible. Is this greed or need?

Greed can cause individuals to lie, cheat, say things not normally said, or commit acts not normally engaged in. Greed may cause people not to tell the whole truth or only part of it and in the process raise their position and let others take the blame. Greed is an ever-present factor or force in many lives.

One person's need is another's greed. Where can the line be drawn? Is one person worth millions of dollars a year because he or she sings differently, performs an athletic feat better than most, or paints a "better" picture? Is it wiser to keep crown jewels for viewing or sell them to provide homes and food for the needy?

GREED AND ETHICS

Greed is not a symptom unique to current society. History shows that as long as the past has been recorded, greed has been present.

Greed can cause people to ignore or bypass personal codes of ethics through a rationalization process. Most codes of ethics make reference to honesty and the necessity of treating others in a just and fair manner. Yet society is inundated with reports of public officials who by accepting "gifts" of paid vacations, use of automobiles, free travel for fact-finding junkets, use of corporate jets, liquor, and in some instances unsecured loans or gifts given under the name of campaign funds violate the trust of those who have elected them to office. (In 1994 the U.S. Senate approved a near-total ban on gifts to members of Congress, but only after three days of bitter debate ["Senate approves near-total," 1994].)

There are those who receive "insider information" concerning future land acquisition by municipalities, state, and federal governments, and advance crop and weather information. Such information can give them a distinct advantage when purchasing land or when investing in the stock or commodities market. With such advance information, large profits are harvested. Or is that just good business?

Greed not only affects politicians, corporations, and professions. It can influence decisions we all make. Too often when an opportunity for financial gain or political power occurs, people are willing to compromise their honor, principles, and reputations.

GREED AND VALUES

Greed can easily affect values because our values are not as deeply seated nor as subject to change as are morals and ethics. Things such as cheating on an exam, short-changing a person, passing shoddy merchandise off as quality goods, or plagiarism of written and recorded material can be affected by greed.

Those who have "different" values find no difficulty in rationalizing their behavior, especially if it can be justified by a difference in values.

An opportunity for quick gain can catch individuals unaware when values such as fairness, respect, trustworthiness, responsibility, or a caring nature are involved. Decisions are justified by our saying, "No one will ever know" or "The risk is slight, I will chance it just this once." Examples include padding an insurance claim, trying to gain favor with an acquaintance by gossiping about a friend, or in the case of younger people, being willing to sacrifice the trust of a parent.

Other examples include salespersons who sell friends more insurance than they can afford or mechanics who charge for parts and repairs that are not needed. Worst of all are those who abuse friendship and trust for personal advancement and gain.

Greed can upset an entire way of life. In his book *The gift of Good Land*, Wendell Berry (1981) reports the plight of Peruvian farmers, who have been raising potatoes high in the Andes for centuries. Their fields were once small and terraced to reduce wind and water erosion. They planted a variety of potatoes to ensure that some survived the weather, disease, and insects.

But several years ago a new, larger hybrid potato, a potato much more desirable for exporting, one with a much higher yield, replaced the traditional varieties. Exports increased and terraces were removed to allow for the use of machinery. As a result, fewer farmers were needed; many moved to the crowded cities and were unable to find work. Wind and water erosion increased, and the farms that once supported many, now support few.

GREED AND MORALS

For some, greed has had a definite effect on socially accepted morals. For example, David McCullough (1992) in his book *Truman* made reference to friends of President Truman who used their appointed positions in government to "peddle" influence. Regarding one of his appointments Truman wrote in his diary:

Since childhood at my mother's knee, I have believed in honor, ethics, and right living as its own reward. I find a *very* small minority who agree with me on that premise. For instance, I picked a West Pointer, son of an honorable father, a man who should have had Washington, Lee, Jackson, Gustavus Adolphus for his ideals, to associate with me in carrying out a program and I got—a dud, a weakling, no ideals, no nothing. He'd use his office for his own enrichment. . . . He'd sell me or anyone else he's associated with out for his own gain. (pp. 185–186)

There are people who are amoral or without morals. Such people have no adherence to any code of ethics other than their own. They take what is wanted by any means. One has to question the greed, morals, and morality of those who, for example, sell mood-altering substances like crack to pregnant women, especially when those doing the dealing know the children will be addicted, born as crack babies.

Once greed prompts a person to compromise his or her ethics, it is easier to compromise the second time.

SUMMARY

Sequestering more than is necessary for a "normal" quality of life, greed is usually thought of in relation to money. It can, however, be a lust for influence and social acceptance.

Greed affects the poor and the rich. That some have so much and others so little has probably never occurred to many of the most wealthy individuals. They can afford their affluent lifestyle, so why not have the very best of everything? Many may also believe that if others shared their work ethic, they could live just as well.

An ever-present choice, greed is behind many problems encountered in society. It acts on the conscious and the subconscious and challenges us to forego that which is right. It influences our decisions at any time. Greed is a powerful force few of us totally escape.

7 _____

Ethics

> When we are shocked by the behaviors of other peoples, it is usually because we erroneously assume that they have our experience and background. (Nida, 1954, p. 36)

Mr. Johnson, returning early to his classroom, found two of his best students working at his desk. They were writing in a notebook, and when finished, returned some papers to the desk drawer—the drawer containing a test to be given later in the day.

The more he thought about this incident, the more concerned he became. The problem was solved by reordering test questions.

Later, when correcting exams, he noted that the two students, found at his desk earlier, did poorly. Upon closer examination, he discovered they had identical answers on most of the matching and true-false questions. Mr. Johnson confronted them. After a period of fidgeting and a period of silence, they broke into tears and admitted cheating on the exam. Mr. Johnson, feeling he had no alternative but to enforce the established policy for cheating, gave them a "zero" on the exam.

This situation was assumed settled until the father of one of the girls confronted Mr. Johnson. He demanded that they be allowed to retake the test, "because a 'zero' grade would all but eliminate their chances of graduating with honors." Mr. Johnson refused. The father, a very influential person in the community, then instructed the principal to either make Mr. Johnson change the scores or to change them himself. The principal gave in and changed the test scores.

Mr. Johnson, a nontenured first-year teacher was not offered a contract for the following year.

There are many different ways, based upon how a situation is perceived and interpreted, to define personal ethics. If you were a member of Mr. Johnson's community, how would you view what transpired in this true situation? Listed below are five possibilities:

1. The principal has no choice in the matter. If he permits this story to get out, the whole community will become involved. Better nip this one in the bud and establish some ground rules for the rest of the faculty.
2. Obviously the students are wrong. They were cheating and everyone knows that it is not tolerated. The fact they were good students has nothing to do with the situation.
3. It is apparent the teacher should have reconsidered his position. Didn't he know enough not to make waves? He could have retested them and no one would have known the difference.
4. Teachers are troublemakers and don't know their place in this community. Get rid of that teacher before he gets tenure and really becomes a problem.
5. The whole thing is ridiculous. They are good girls. It was done as a lark, and besides, the desk drawer wasn't even locked. In the final analysis, what difference does it make?

DEFINITION OF ETHICS

Ethics is the branch of philosophy that deals with right and wrong, good and bad, or in a religious sense, with righteousness and evil. Ethics are rules to live by, rules to guide behavior. Ethics describe what the world should be like, not how it is. Another view of ethics is that they are guidelines: Guidelines modeled or taught by parents, friends, teachers, peers, and people whom we respect and want to emulate.

Philosophers develop their own philosophies of ethics based upon the society in which they live, their own education, their personal wealth, and their concept of what constitutes ethical practices and behavior. Let's consider a few such philosophies of ethics.

Looking at ethics in a formal way, Mackenzie (1925) said, "Ethics is the science which deals with the Ideal, or with the Standard of Rightness and Wrongness, Good and Evil in Conduct" (p. 1).

Brown (1991) suggests that ethics assumes that "people have the freedom and power to respond—that is, options, the freedom and power to consider different options, to analyze the options, strengths and weaknesses, and to choose one option over the others based on its merits. These assumptions provide a way of looking at situations and responding to the various parties involved" (p. 16).

Sharma (1965) presents ethics as a "philosophy of life" and asks us to consider "what type of behavior or conduct can be regarded as moral and what kind of conduct is immoral" (p. 29). He states that ethics "discriminates between the right and the wrong and the good and the evil, and points out what is the supreme good towards which all our life is to be directed.... From this point of view, it can be said that ethics is a philosophy of life" (p. 44).

As can be seen, there are many different views and definitions of ethics. Each of us, when pondering which ethical viewpoint or philosophy to accept, will probably do pretty much what philosophers do, select one based largely upon our own personal background, education, and the influence our family has had upon us. We will then use that philosophy in developing our own personal concept of ethics.

HISTORY OF ETHICS

For as long as people have spoken and lived in tribes and societies, there have probably been philosophers. Recorded dissertations on ethics date back to the fourth century B.C., when Plato chronicled speeches of Socrates in addition to his own.

European philosophy continued with the Romans and the early Christians. Philosophical thought was kept alive and grew in the libraries and centers of learning built and maintained by the Moors in North Africa and in Spain. Early Christian monks living in secluded monasteries preserved earlier documents. For about 1,000 years (A.D. 500–1500) philosophical thought had limited growth outside the clergy. The growth of ethics and other philosophical points of view became the domain of the church during the Dark Ages. Sidgwick (1965) elaborated: "In the 15th century the sway of medieval thought is assailed and undermined by the Renaissance; in the 16th the Reformation and the growth of physical science combine to shatter it; with the 17th century the period of modern thought has effectively begun" (p. xxii). Since the 17th century, many people, philosophers, educators, theologians among them, have felt free to voice their opinions and understanding of ethics.

There is insufficient space to mention all individuals who contributed to the development of ethics. A few of the more significant are discussed briefly in the following pages.

Aristotle (388–322 B.C.) and others of his time followed and taught the concept of virtue. Their concept of ethics, called *virtue ethics*, was based upon the idea that "virtue was goodness or excellence in all human functions, both in thought, and of action, in individual conduct in civic life" (Banner, 1968, p. 168). Aristotle and his contemporaries also discussed the concept of a spirit separate from the body, even a "life" after death, possibly reincarnation as a continuation of life's "spirit." Much later theologians interpreted the spirit as the "soul," with the idea of an afterlife (heaven) being a reward for how one had lived his or her life on earth. Thus, religion entered the field of philosophy and ethics.

St. Thomas of Aquinas (1224–1274) patterned much of his philosophical writings after those of Aristotle. His form of ethical teaching is called by many *natural form ethics*. "For St. Thomas, all individuals, as rational beings, are capable of knowing the law of nature and of obeying its precepts" (Banner, 1968, p. 85).

Later Immanual Kant (1724–1804), a German philosopher, dealt with moral philosophy. His branch of moral philosophy is called *deontological ethics*. This differed from the virtue ethics of Aristotle and the natural form ethics of St. Thomas of Aquinas in that it proposes that "the only motive for obeying the rules necessary to social life is the pleasure to be found in obedience or the pain resulting from disobedience" (MacIntyer, 1966, p. 235). Kant also held that "moral reasoning should be based on whether the moral principle or rule in question can be ethically justified on its own . . . that the principle or rule must pass moral muster independent of whether good consequences will likely follow from adhering to it" (Ashmore & Starr, 1991, p. 26).

John Mills (1806–1873), a nineteenth-century British philosopher writing a century after Kant, was a strong proponent of *utilitarian ethics*. "This theory holds that one ought to do that which will provide the greatest benefit for society" (Ashmore & Starr, 1991, p. 30).

A more recent entrant into the ethics debate is the *existentialist* point of view. The rise of existentialism to a place of prominence in philosophical thought occurred during the late nineteenth century and continued into the twentieth century. The writings of Jean-Paul Sartre and Soren Kierkegaard influenced many, including Carl Rogers and A. S. Neil, by presenting the theory that anything that represses the rights of individuals is a negative influence and such negative influences might even be considered unethical.

Kimbrough (1985) wrote, "Existentialists are free to make the right decisions as long as they are responsible, the decisions are free of external restraints, and they are willing to stand accountable for their decisions" (p. 43).

Anderson et al. (1992) explain:

Humans . . . must be taught to have courage and independence, for it is much easier to fear freedom and live by directions, sanctions, and ethical principles handed down from on high than it is to be aware that every word and every deed is a choice and that we must decide what to believe and what propositions are meaningful and significant. Existentialists believe that all of life is ad-lib, that we are given a script with blank pages, and that we become what we conceive ourselves to be. They believe that either we make ourselves or allow others to decide how we should live our only life. (p. 32)

SELECTING AN ETHICAL PHILOSOPHY

Most people at some time in their lives are exposed to ethics. Ethical situations may have been discussed in a twelfth-grade philosophy class or in a college honors section, preached in a sermon, explained by a parent or grandparent, learned through a business transaction, or learned by carefully observing a productive, sensitive human being.

Unfortunately, some only observe ethical decisions being modeled by those whose decisions are based upon who is watching, not upon a philosophy of ethics.

With all of the different interpretations and definitions of ethics espoused by philosophers, its study can pose problems for the average person because there are a variety of different ethical points of view from which to choose.

For instance, after reading a portion of Plato's *Republic* and concepts of an ideal society governed by just individuals, one might easily identify with Plato's views, especially now when so many politicians have been shown to have feet of clay. Likewise, with the writings of Aristotle and the Epicureans, which maintained that a virtuous life is a happy life, their views will perhaps hold much meaning for those who are good, law-abiding citizens.

The views of St. Thomas of Aquinas, a Roman Catholic religious leader who agreed with St. Augustine, a fourth-century Christian priest, are that "the individual's good, in this life, is the contemplation of God joined together with the exercise of prudence and benevolence in practical affairs, as after death the individual's good is the enjoyment of God Himself" (Banner, 1968, p. 80). His views may well have a profound effect on persons with a strong religious ethic.

Those who attended a more rigid private or public school with a strong formal curriculum or have found security and order in military service, even those growing up in a family with strict rules, might be impressed with and accept Kant's view of "duty as being an ethical fundamental."

With the patience and tenacity to absorb the writings of Sartre and Kierkegaard, one might find kindred spirits in the idea that people should make decisions based upon what is best for them and society, not what is best for politicians, big business, and power brokers.

The list of ethical philosophies from which one might select a single one to follow is lengthy. It becomes more difficult to select a specific ethical point of view as philosophers begin to combine terminology, for example, ethical values and moral ethics. Consequently, many people solve the problem of searching for an ethical philosophy to guide their lives by either (1) dropping the search and choosing to emulate someone whom they like and respect or (2) forming an *eclectic* philosophy, a composite developed by choosing portions of different philosophies of ethics.

Belok, Bontrager, Oswald, Morris, and Erickson (1966) elaborated upon this dilemma when discussing ethical systems.

All ethical systems (generalizations or principles preferred by any groups as guides to conduct) have this in common; they reflect some beliefs about the nature of people and the nature of the universe. In a sense, the moral and spiritual values of a culture may be regarded as predictions which hold that if we follow certain prescribed codes of conduct, beneficent consequences will follow. They also serve the useful function of enabling one individual to predict what another individual in the culture will do, how he will behave under certain circumstances. . . . A human ethical system (animals can have no ethical system) must therefore be based on correct assessment of what contributes the external environment states for the human class of life. (p. 247)

In deciding upon which ethical philosophy to select and follow, one discovers that the concept of ethics is just as applicable to large groups of people (for example, governments) as to individuals.

In summary, throughout recorded history philosophers have debated how one can identify right from wrong and good from bad. This is because ethics as a philosophical field is not exact, precise, or absolute. (If it were, there would not be such a proliferation of philosophical points of view.) It is important to remember that selecting a personal ethical philosophy helps people make rational decisions based upon something other than whim.

U.S. ETHICAL RESPONSES TO PROBLEMS IN EDUCATION

Ethical behavior and decision making applies to governments as well as to individuals. Governments should respond to the needs of the citizens, representing the will of the majority. Governments, however, move slowly. Eventually, though, through the efforts and actions of persistent ethical people, governments do respond.

Some of the more notable situations requiring ethical decisions the United States has addressed have related to education. One of the most far-reaching was "separate but equal schools" (*Plessy vs. Ferguson*, 1896). In 1954, a decision by the U.S. Supreme Court did away with separate but equal schools (*Brown vs. the Board of Education of Topeka*).

This was followed by the Civil Rights Act of 1964, which prohibited discrimination in public accommodations, employment practices, *and* education. The Supreme Court also provided for federal enforcement of laws against discrimination through the courts. Gutek (1983) wrote: "Of particular importance in education was the provision that prohibited discrimination in programs that were federally funded. School districts and educational institutions which violated the nondiscrimination provisions of the act could lose federal funds" (p. 96).

In 1968 the Supreme Court ruled that school district policies allowing students the option of transferring from one school district to another to avoid desegregation were unconstitutional (*Green vs. County School Board;*

Monroe vs. Board of Commonwealth). In 1971 the Supreme Court upheld the use of citywide busing to force integration of schools.

Other examples of ethical responses to discrimination in education are two federal laws written especially for children with special needs. One is the Vocational Rehabilitation Act of 1973 (PL 93–516), which transferred the Rehabilitation Services Administration to the office of the Secretary of Health, Education, and Welfare, strengthened programs for the blind, and provided for the convening of the White House Conference on Handicapped Individuals. The second is Public Law 94–142, which was established to meet the needs of individuals between the ages of three and twenty-one (Education for All Handicapped Children Act, 1975). It provided for vocational training in mainstream settings and promotion and expansion of employment opportunities, and it called for the removal of architectural and transportation barriers.

CODES OF ETHICS

A *code of ethics* is a set of rules of conduct that suggest how people should conduct themselves in respect to right and to wrong behavior, decisions regarding relationships with others, and, in a religious context, how to conduct themselves in respect to righteous and evil behavior. Most professions have adopted a code of ethics to guide members and direct their actions. A code of ethics usually includes standards of proper conduct. The Hippocratic Oath, Hammurabi's Code, the Babylonian Code, and Moses' Ten Commandments are examples of early codes.

Codes of ethics are developed to give direction and to act as guidelines for groups of people. These guidelines focus upon making us better citizens. They also help us make ethical decisions regarding how we work with individuals and how we live our lives in social groups. Codes of ethics offer few problems for conformists.

Codes of ethics also may stipulate what one should refrain from doing as a member of a particular profession or group. Some codes have penalties for noncompliance that could lead to loss of membership privileges, even to the loss of licensure.

Government Codes of Ethics

The call for ethics in professional life has become more pronounced as the public has become increasingly aware of scandals, abuse of public office, and corruption by persons in positions of authority. Many professions and businesses, and even the federal government, have become conscious of how they are perceived ethically by their constituents. Some, in turn, have appointed "agency ethics officials" to help employees *and* management determine which acts may be considered unethical.

In 1989 President Bush charged the Office of Government Ethics to create a comprehensive, objective, reasonable, and enforceable set of executive branch standards of conduct. The order resulted in a document about ethics for all executive branch employees entitled *Take the High Road* (1993). This document identifies situations in which employees might find themselves, situations where they may need help in making ethical decisions. It offers interpretations concerning what is ethical and unethical conduct. Areas considered are gifts from outside sources, gifts between employees, conflicting financial interests, impartiality in performing public duties, seeking other employment, restrictions placed on former employees, and other nonrelated outside activities (hobbies, part-time work to supplement income, representing clients on matters not related to government work, or involvement in an enterprise that does business with the government). The same document was used by the Department of Defense, with a few additions for military personnel. Included in the Department of Defense code of ethics publication for the U.S. Army are the "Principles of Ethical Conduct" (*Command information packet*, 1993).

Government agencies, whose existence and support depend upon money raised by taxation and allocated by legislation, are very concerned with their professional image and ethical standards.

Business Codes of Ethics

Codes of ethics for those in the field of business are usually less well defined and less specific than other professional codes. Benson (1982) defines business codes of ethics as "those principles, or aspirations towards principles, that guided most or at least some businessmen in their commercial connections" (p. 4). Bowie & Duska (1990) elaborate upon business codes of ethics: "The word ethics refers to many things; a code of rules, a set of principles one lives by, or the study of what is right or wrong. . . . Simply put, ethics, for our purposes, is a study that attempts to shed light on the question 'What should one do?' " (p. 3).

The purpose for codes of ethics in business and in government is similar. Codes of ethics help guide individual and group decision making and behavior. Thus, the focus of ethics for businesses tends to emphasize human actions and behaviors. Since business transactions are based upon the buying and selling of goods, services, and information, drawing the line between good business practices and ethical behavior sometimes becomes difficult. That makes business ethics more difficult to define and adhere to. Does insider information in a business transaction constitute an unfair advantage? Is the withholding of information ethical even if the client is satisfied? Does the expression "Let the buyer beware" have any place in an ethical business transaction? Is industrial espionage justified ethical behavior? Such questions have provided the basis for many legal and legislative battles not only in the business profession but in the governmental area as well.

In conclusion, the success of a business is very dependent upon how it is perceived. If the perception is one of trust, one that creates positive feelings, and one of good will, customers will be retained.

Education Codes of Ethics

Education involves students and adults, including administrators, teachers, secretaries, custodians, cooks, and paraprofessionals, in leadership *and* modeling roles. The education profession is indirectly concerned with ethics at national, state, local, and personal levels. Educators are constantly making ethical decisions, taking into consideration their students' socioeconomic, academic, and ethnic backgrounds. Educators continually make decisions involving right or wrong, good or bad. All these decisions dramatically affect the end product of education, the student.

Consequently, codes of ethics for administrators, teachers, librarians, and school board members have been developed. For example, in 1976 the National Education Association (NEA) developed for its membership a code of ethics that contains two principles—a commitment to the student and a commitment to the profession. The commitment to the student states: "The educator strives to help each student realize his or her potential as a worthy and effective member of society. The educator therefore works to stimulate the spirit of inquiry, the acquisition of knowledge and understanding, and the thoughtful formulation of worthy goals" (pp. 376–377). In addition, the NEA code lists eight "shall nots" for educators.

The section in the code of ethics that addresses the commitment of teachers to the teaching profession states:

The education profession is vested by the public with a trust and responsibility requiring the highest ideals of professional service. In the belief that the quality of the services of the education profession directly influences the nation and its citizens, the educator shall exert every effort to raise professional standards, to promote a climate that encourages the exercise of professional judgment, to achieve conditions that attract persons worthy of the trust to careers in education, and to assist in preventing the practice of the profession by unqualified persons. (*National Education Association code of ethics*, 1993, pp. 376–377)

Most states have developed codes of ethics for public school teachers. For example, the code for Minnesota teachers was developed by the Minnesota Board of Teaching (MBT), a group of educators and citizens appointed by the governor. The Code of Ethics for Minnesota Teachers begins by stating:

Each teacher, upon entering the teaching profession, assumes a number of obligations, one of which is to adhere to a set of principles which defines professional
conduct. These principles are reflected in the following code of ethics, which sets
forth to the education profession and the public it serves standards of professional
conduct and procedures for implementation. ("The code of ethics for Minnesota
teachers," 1994)

The MBT code then identifies ten standards of professional conduct that
must be followed. The standards are as follows:

A. A teacher shall provide professional educational services in a nondiscrimina-
    tory manner.
B. A teacher shall make reasonable effort to protect the student from conditions
    harmful to health and safety.
C. In accordance with state and federal laws, a teacher shall disclose confidential
    information about individuals only when a compelling professional purpose
    is served or when required by law.
D. A teacher shall take reasonable disciplinary action in exercising the authority
    to provide an atmosphere conducive to learning.
E. A teacher shall not use professional relationships with students, parents, and
    colleagues to private advantage.
F. A teacher shall delegate authority for teaching responsibilities only to licensed
    personnel.
G. A teacher shall not deliberately suppress or distort subject matter.
H. A teacher shall not knowingly falsify or misrepresent records or facts relating
    to that teacher's own qualifications or to other teachers' qualifications.
I. A teacher shall not knowingly make false or malicious statements about
    students or colleagues.
J. A teacher shall accept a contract for a teaching position that requires licensing
    only if properly or provisionally licensed for that position. (1994)

"The Code of Ethics for Minnesota Teachers" also identifies (1) procedures to be followed when complaints are investigated and (2) policies to
be enforced if the code has been violated. Punishment for violation of the
code of ethics may result in a letter of censure from the MBT, suspension of
license, or revocation of a license to teach.

The latest code of ethics for school administrators was approved by the
American Association of School Administrators in 1976. It also contains a
list of ten standards to be followed by its membership.

Most school districts also have a code of ethics for members of local
boards of education. Such codes generally include identifying (1) how
members will act during their tenure on the board, (2) their function as
board members, (3) procedures for working effectively with other board
members, and (4) their responsibility for working with the superintendent
of schools and other school officials.

One of the more brief codes is that of the American Library Association. In six short statements it identifies the duties, responsibilities, patrons' right to privacy, need to work cooperatively with others in spite of personal philosophical differences, and necessity of avoiding conflicts of interest while on the job.

Strike and Soltis (1985) used the NEA's code of ethics to illustrate their concept of ethics and educators. They said, "We are less concerned with your learning the code than in getting you to think about ethics and educating on your own. Ethical thinking and decision making are not just following the rules" (p. 3). Strike and Soltis's book *The Ethics of Teaching* is an excellent example of the application of ethical thinking and decision making for educators. In a similar context, Kimbrough (1985), when writing about administrators and ethical decision making, suggested, "An ethicist [one who studies ethics] must not be bound by customs and traditions. Indeed, neither ethicists, nor school administrators, can depend on custom as a source of ethics because change is inevitable and always influences ethical decisions" (p. 47).

Strike, Soltis, and Kimbrough see ethical behavior as something that can be discussed, modeled, taught, and learned by others. They see ethics as being fluid. They also see it as a reflection of our changing school population, that is, the faculty, parents, staff workers, and administrators as well as the students. Ethics in education reflects an amalgamation of ideas, methodologies, and teaching and learning strategies tempered by the belief systems of the school district's constituents. Educators should consider all ethical belief systems, including their own, when developing curriculum, responding to student needs, and establishing ethical codes for students and staff. Simon et al. (1972) conclude, "Ethics concerns what kinds of actions are right or wrong, what kind of life is a good life, or what kind of person is a good person. . . . Ethical claims . . . do not tell us how the world is but how it ought to be" (p. 7).

In summary, for all who work in education codes of ethics are essential. They remind educators that it is necessary for those who work with children to set positive examples and to model ethical behavior.

ETHICS AND TEACHING

How does one teach ethical behavior? How can a person convince another individual that right is better than wrong, even if they can agree upon a definition of right and wrong? The truth is, not all will accept the proposal that right is better than wrong. Not all are ready—some must suffer first. History documents the price of anarchy, greed, and misdirected influence. As rulers are disposed, as countries fall, as leaders are replaced, it is the citizens who suffer from such actions.

The world of science operates by rules—of gravity, density, displacement, the temperature necessary for an element to change from a solid, to a liquid, to a gas. There are also accepted universal laws in science and mathematics. Like science, society and human endeavor have rules, stated in codes of ethics. These codes show how good life can be if people adhere to the rules.

For those who follow rules of business, laws of science, or standards of a profession, outcomes tend to be predictable. Science, math, foreign languages, business, and engineering are examples of disciplines where outcomes can be projected with reasonable accuracy if rules are followed.

Yet human sciences, also, have a degree of predictability. History, for example, is a predictor if used with discretion because if we study the history of civilizations, we find people making the same mistakes of judgment over and over. Often humans become beset with greed, self-importance, and poor insight into their own action and behavior. All too frequently, humans think only of themselves.

Educators can demonstrate and project ethical outcomes that assist decision making. Teachers can model and demonstrate ethical qualities and decision-making skills. In the final analysis, however, it is the student who will make the decision to accept the entire concept of ethical practice, accept part of it, or reject the principle.

In order to flourish a society requires the participation of a majority of those willing to act in the best interest of all who form the society. When greed, selfishness, and personal pleasure supersede, any society is subject to collapse.

SUMMARY

Ethics are standards by which people live. All theories of ethics have their disciples, willing to defend the views they hold. Codes of ethics are guidelines for members of a profession or organization. Their purpose is to help identify behavior, decisions, and actions considered ethical.

As educators we must be aware of the differences as well as the similarities students bring into our schools. To influence students at a time when they are receptive, we must continually teach and reteach important ethical concepts and at the same time model and demonstrate ethical behavior.

You may write to the addresses listed below to obtain copies of codes of ethics for the following organizations

Code of Ethics of the American Library Association
American Library Association
50 E. Huron St.
Chicago, IL 60611

Ethics for Army Personnel
Command Information Package
"The Army Focuses on Ethics"

HQDA (SAPA-CI/CIP)
Office of the Chief of Public Affairs
1500 Army Pentagon 2d622
Washington, DC 20310–1500

Code of Ethics for Minnesota Teachers
Executive Secretary
Minnesota Board of Teaching
608 Capitol Square Building
550 Cedar Street
St. Paul, MN 55101

Government Code of Ethics
Ethics Booklet for Executive Branch Employees
"Take the High Road"
U.S. Government Printing Office
Mail Stop: SSOP
Washington, DC 20402–9328

Code of Ethics for School Board Members
National School Boards Association
1680 Duke St.
Alexandria, VA 22314

Code of Ethics of the NEA
National Education Association
1201 16th St. N.W.
Washington, DC 20036

Ethics for School Administrators
American Association of School Administrators
1801 N. Moore St.
Arlington, VA 22209

8

Values

If traditional values aren't taught, the space in the human mind they would occupy does not remain empty. It fills up with other ideas, the kind that lead to the ruinous choices so many young people are making. (Ward, 1993, p. 4)

All people have values. It doesn't matter whether people are rich or poor, famous or infamous, geniuses or unable to read or write. Values may be positive or negative, shared by a single person or by many. Each person defines values based upon his or her culture, age, sex, and philosophical beliefs.

Shaver and Strong (1982) suggest that "values are the criteria by which we judge things to be good, worthwhile, desirable or bad, worthless, despicable or somewhere in between the two extremes" (p. 17). They state that there is no sense in pretending any definition is correct.

Eyre and Eyre (1993) say, "By values we mean the standards of our actions and attitudes of our hearts and minds that shape who we are, how we live, and how we treat other people" (p. 15).

Other definitions refer to values as being the worth a person places on a concept worthy of following. Values may also be defined as guidelines and beliefs individuals hold to be true. They may also be defined as guidelines that aid and direct the making of daily and long-range decisions, especially those pertaining to how we should respond to individuals and groups that make up the society in which we live.

Thornburgh (1991) suggests: "Sometimes we think laws and values are the same. They're related but they're not the same. We establish laws to codify certain rules and standards that allow us to live together peacefully as a free people. But it's our values that inspire our laws—not our laws that establish our values. Laws tell us what we *must* do. Values summon us to what we *should* do" (p. 205).

Personal frames of reference influence what is considered to be of value. Factors such as peer pressure, parental modeling, hero emulation, or an act that impresses a person also influence development and formation of personal values. As individuals, each of us develops his or her own value system, one that allows us to function in society.

Value formation begins in infancy and is changed, modified, or discarded as people pass through the various stages of life—childhood, adolescence, adulthood, and old age.

When most humans live within a small society, community, or group, values are shared. The smaller, more tightly knit the group, the more similar the values. As societies become more pluralistic, especially as they are in the United States, where the citizens represent many ethnic and socioeconomic backgrounds, an opportunity for greater exposure to a wider range of group and individual values exists.

During the latter half of the nineteenth century, people from many countries emigrated to America, often settling in communities or parts of cities where they found familiarity and security, sharing common religious, cultural, and political heritages. The values of parents and the community were passed down through each generation and became the values held by their children. As improved transportation reduced isolation between rural areas and cities, and as national borders no longer separated and isolated groups, people worked together, traded merchandise, and shared ideas. People became exposed to new and different values. Some were rejected, others accepted.

HISTORY OF VALUES TEACHING IN THE UNITED STATES

Early in the history of the United States one of the primary goals of education was the teaching of reading so that each individual could read the Bible, the one, if not the only, book found in most homes. Consequently, the Bible was used as a source to teach reading and subsequently values. Later, as the country become more populated with people of different religions, arguments arose as to which version of the Bible should be used. Much of the controversy was put to rest with the publication of a series of reading books "made especially to meet the needs of the great civilization developing in the Ohio country" (Minnich, 1936, p. 32). They were written by William Holmes McGuffey, a Presbyterian minister and university professor whose *Primer* was first published in 1836. The series contained lessons in values and morals, in addition to heroic tales and poetry, but it did not represent a specific version of the Bible. Thus, the McGuffey Reader series became one of the best-selling reading series of the nineteenth century. It was reprinted many times between 1836 and 1920 by seven different publishing companies. (It was even reprinted and offered for sale in many of the John Birch Society bookstores during the latter part of the twentieth century.)

In his series McGuffey emphasized, in story form, qualities and behaviors such as kindness, honesty, goodness, promptness, and truthfulness, as well as reverence and piety (Minnich, 1936).

Following the Civil War the population of the United States increased, largely through immigration, as did the population of public schools. Now the question became one of whose values should be taught, rather than which version of the Bible should be used. Also, questions arose about other parts of the curriculum, such as the importance of subjects like Greek and Latin, holdovers from the classical curriculum. The teaching of values, Greek, and Latin lost its place in the curriculum as more time was devoted to subjects such as mathematics, science, literature, and modern foreign languages.

The last half of the twentieth century saw the reemergence of values education in the public schools. It appeared in the form of values clarification—a concern "with techniques for stimulating students to think about and clarify their own values" (Shaver & Strong, 1982, p. 136). The origin of values clarification began with the work of Louis Raths. Raths, and colleagues Merrill Harmin and Sidney Simon, published their views in a book entitled *Values and Teaching: Working with Values in the Classroom* (1966). Later, in 1972, Sidney Simon, Leland Howe, and Howard Kirschenbaum published a handbook for students and teachers called *Values Clarification: A Handbook of Practical Strategies for Teachers and Students*. It contains seventy-nine classroom strategies for helping students become more aware of their own values. Some of their strategies include such things as identifying twenty things you like to do, completing a values survey, writing "I Wonder" statements, practicing brainstorming, conducting a pattern search, and identifying "Who Are You" statements (Simon, Howe, & Kirschenbaum, 1972).

UNIVERSAL VALUES

Most people would agree values such as honor, character, virtue, courage, hard work, thrift, sharing, and family are acceptable by the vast majority. Such values, when widely accepted, are referred to as universal values.

Other universal values are knowledge, social responsibility, and sincerity. Very few question such values. Questions are raised, however, about the personal values of teachers who would conduct classes about values. Whose values should be taught? Would they instruct their students in selecting those values supported by the district or would they, as teachers, feel compelled to include their own? In essence, this is a dichotomy because it is virtually impossible to teach any subject to anyone without consciously, or especially subconsciously, expressing and modeling personal values.

WHERE VALUES TEACHING BEGINS

A child begins to form values at a very young age, possibly before he or she can speak. A child responds when held, nourished, cuddled, or sung to long before learning to talk or walk. Children usually respond to such affection by laughing, cooing, and smiling. As they mature, they watch the behavior of others around them and observe how they respond or react to anger, fear, love, affection, crisis, and conflict. They are constantly assimilating impressions as to how they might respond to similar situations. At the same time values are being formed. Often, when children misbehave, they are using coping skills that have been modeled for them either intentionally or unintentionally.

As parents, siblings, friends, relatives, and others act and react, youngsters are observing and determining the worth of the values being demonstrated. If someone whom they respect places value on an act, an object, or a personal trait, youngsters are likely to accept that act, object, or trait as valuable and will likely make similar decisions regarding what to include within their personal value system.

As children grow older, they assume or accept the values of friends and acquaintances. The sphere of influence may extend to popular entertainers, athletes, or even cartoon characters. Young people observe behavior, see it being accepted by others, and then model it.

Modeling can be both positive and negative, good or bad, or somewhere in between. Children observe their role model(s) and begin to develop a value system of their own. They observe how conflict is handled and see the respect or lack of respect a parent or sibling has for others in the family. They note cooperation at home and at school. Young people observe examples of fairness, respect, manners, and politeness. They see socioeconomic, ethnic, and religious tolerance or intolerance for others. Children develop a concept of honesty and trustworthiness based upon how they themselves are treated and trusted.

Children are not aware of forming values or the process involved, yet it occurs nevertheless. How is responsibility within the family handled? Is it shared, delegated, or ignored? How is love, trust, joy, and caring modeled? Is there respect for individual differences?

Have young people within the family been exposed to concepts of duty, reverence, and an understanding of other people's needs? Has the art of compromise ever been modeled for them as a solution for handling conflict? Eyre and Eyre (1993) write:

With or without their parents' help, children will begin developing both conscious and subconscious values during preschool years. They learn partly from their friends, partly from television, but mostly from their family. They test and develop and sometimes alter these values as they enter school. As they approach adolescence, they struggle for autonomy and begin to set up their own value system, which is independent of (but not usually very different from) that of their parents.

If their parents avoid educating them regarding values, they'll learn—primarily—that values aren't important. (p. 22)

This poses a problem for many children because our society is struggling with the concept of what constitutes a family. The concept of a traditional family of mother, father, and two children has changed. So has the fact that one parent will be home to model proper values. A family today can be the child and one parent, the child living with relatives such as grandparents, or the child living with aunts and uncles or older brothers and sisters; possibly a family can be the one a child finds in a foster home. When it is necessary for the single parent or both parents to work, children too young for school are usually placed in either day care or preschool, left with a hired sitter, or left with older family members. What parenting skills are being modeled by those acting as substitute parents?

When children enter school, teachers may spend more time with them than their parents. Thus, teachers must recognize both the opportunity and the responsibility they have for being positive role models. As the child progresses through school, becoming more involved in extracurricular activities, clubs, and organizations, forces outside the family sphere exert more and more influence. Peer pressure becomes much more influential than the family. Selecting which values to follow and use can be very confusing to children.

REINTRODUCING VALUES INTO THE CURRICULUM

There are many reasons for reintroducing the teaching of values into the school curriculum. One of the most important is that people—parents, teachers, even those who have no children of their own—feel it is necessary in our changing society to ensure that acceptable, universal values are presented to children at a time when they are most impressionable.

Evidence shows that the public would like to see the teaching of values reinstated in the public school curriculum, and the best evidence we have is the results of the Twenty-fifth Annual Phi Delta Kappa Gallop Poll. Phi Delta Kappa, a professional fraternity in education, conducts an annual poll on the public's attitudes toward the public schools. A cross section of the adult population in the United States has been polled annually. In the 1993 poll two specific questions were asked. First, "Do you think it would be possible, or not possible, to get people in your community to agree on a set of basic values, such as honesty and patriotism, that would be taught in the local public schools?" The answer revealed by the poll showed that 73 percent of public and private school parents interviewed responded positively, while 67 percent of individuals with no children in school responded positively. When the responses of public and private school parents were combined with the responses of individuals with no children in school, 69 percent of those polled responded positively to the question regarding a set of basic values.

The second question was "I am going to read a list of different values that might be taught in the public schools. For each one, please tell me whether you think it should be taught, or should not be taught, to all students in the public schools in your community." Those polled indicated values they felt were most important and should be taught in public schools. The following are in rank order of responses received:

Honesty, 97%

Democracy, 93%;

Acceptance of people of different races and ethnic backgrounds, 93%

Patriotism, love of country, 93%

Caring for friends and family members, 91%

Moral courage, 91%

The golden rule, 90%

Acceptance of people who hold different religious beliefs, 87%

Acceptance of people who hold unpopular or controversial political or social views, 73%

Sexual abstinence outside of marriage, 66%

Acceptance of the right of a woman to choose abortion, 56%

Acceptance of people with different sexual orientations; that is, homosexuals or bisexuals, 51% (Elam, Rose, & Gallop, 1993, p. 145)

The results indicate a strong interest for the public schools to become involved in the teaching of accepted values.

JUSTIFICATION FOR INCLUDING VALUES
IN THE CURRICULUM

What are reasons for reintroducing the teaching of values into the school curriculum? The first is that schools are encountering a rising rate of youth violence. At one time chewing gum, running in the halls, or speaking out of turn were considered to be the main disruptions in school. Now educators face serious problems such as controlling drugs, weapons, and physical assault against students and teachers in elementary and secondary schools. Respect for authority seems to be at an all-time low, not only in schools but in all phases of our society.

A second reason is that if a person reads the daily newspapers or weekly news magazines such as *Time* and *Newsweek* or watches local, national, and international news reports, he or she is aware of the scandals involving prominent governmental officials, stock market manipulation, and national leaders lying or saying they "don't remember." Manufacturers have been accused of marketing goods with built-in hazards to those who use their products. Those convicted of breaking the law by stealing money through manipulation of banking procedures serve limited sentences in minimum-security prisons and manage to retain millions of dollars in ill-gotten funds. This implies that lying, cheating, and stealing pay big dividends in comparison to the penalties.

A third reason for reintroducing values into the school curriculum is because of the vandalism of public and private property that forces us to ask ourselves, "What must people be thinking who deface or destroy the property of others? What kind of people spray-paint satanic symbols, graffiti, and obscene words on walls, on subway cars, and even on the Vietnam Memorial?" We are outraged and would willingly incarcerate those who engage in such behavior if the courts would comply. Yet we accept the pollution of our rivers and the industrial waste that poisons the air we breathe. We accept pollution of our environment with all kinds of advertising, even the possibility of "space billboard" advertising (as mentioned in Chapter 3).

Perhaps value systems can be compromised if jobs and profit are involved.

DISTURBING TRENDS IN OUR SOCIETY

Each day the media reports acts of violence committed by youth. Jean Hopfensperger reported the escalation of children involved in "grown-up crime." For example, in 1992 police in Minnesota made nearly 17,000 arrests of children fourteen years of age or younger. (This is compared to 10,200 in 1980.) More than 900 were children under ten, 4,600 ages ten to twelve, and 11,200 ages thirteen and fourteen. In Hennepin County, which includes the city of Minneapolis, during this same time period nearly 4,500 arrests of children fourteen or younger were made. Nearly 200 of those were ages nine and younger (1994, February 20).

Although delinquent children may appear normal, their stories are not. They commit crimes including shoplifting, sexual abuse, robbery, assault, and even murder. When questioned, many children reveal they have observed such behavior modeled by others in the community, even in their own homes. Many are victims of abuse themselves.

Lack of Honesty

We've all heard stories (some call them myths or tall tales) of George Washington admitting to cutting down his father's cherry tree, and of Abraham Lincoln walking many miles after work to return a few pennies he had overcharged a customer, as well as other stories portraying honesty as a virtue. But today heroes admit to gambling on their own athletic team, lying on income tax forms, or using inside information to manipulate stock purchases. Students at U.S. military academies cheat on exams in spite of the honor code. Those who do not cheat refuse to inform on those who do.

Youth today are not stupid. They observe fraud in the area of securities and taxes, insider trading on the stock market, and other white-collar crimes. And they see that those who are apprehended and proven guilty receive relatively light sentences and manage to keep nearly all the money from their questionable endeavors. It is no wonder young people question the value of honesty.

Disrespect for Authority

Who among us has not cheated on the speed limit, not stopped for a stop sign, or ignored a no-parking zone and hoped to avoid being ticketed? There are those who insist on smoking in nonsmoking areas, parking in handicapped zones, and illegally using other people's telephone numbers for making long-distance calls. Insignificant as they may be in comparison to grosser examples of dishonesty, these acts send a very distinct message to young, impressionable minds. Multiply simple instances such as these and the messages become stronger. All too often we read statements in our newspapers that say, "I shot my parents because they abused me as a child" or "I took the money because I needed it more than the company" or "I robbed the bank because it has lots of money and I do not." Without firm values for a guide, one can rationalize almost any decision.

Bigotry

Accepting people of a different race or religion has always been a problem for some. Those who are strangers are thought of as different and therefore not to be trusted. In what is called the Holy Land and in Northern Ireland there is conflict between different religious groups. It is the same in Pakistan. In South Africa the conflict is between black Africans and white Africans. Each group feels justified in its quest for power and autonomy. In the United States members of the Klu Klux Klan and white Protestant supremacists, holdovers from the post–Civil War period, continue to intimidate by preaching their doctrine of racial and religious purity and by burning crosses on the lawns of black families. One of the newer arrivals on the scene of bigotry is a group known by the name of Skinheads. They seem to epitomize all that the Nazi party stood for.

Bigotry is a very powerful concept in that it builds walls between people, walls that lead to conflict, including warfare. Bigotry is a refusal to communicate, to consider the rights of others, to even consider the values held by others. Bigotry is a powerful, almost fanatical concept because the bigot, like the fanatic, *knows* he or she is right and is willing to prove it by any means necessary.

A Growing Self-Centeredness

Another sign of our times, which demonstrates the lack of values, is the number of people who have withdrawn from community activities. People who were once involved with church projects, community affairs, local politics, school activities, and civil rights activities aimed in reducing racial tensions have opted out. Possibly they have become tired and disillusioned. Possibly they have seen an escalation of harassment and crime in their communities and feel intimidated going to and from these activities.

Marshall Kaplan (1993) suggests we consider the rhetoric that sometimes obscures the real problem. He asks: "Our nation is committed to the value and worth of each human being and to the development of respect for each individual's humanity. Why, then, do we tolerate the pervasive marketing and use of gratuitous sex and violence on television, on records, and in newspapers?" (p. 72A).

SUMMARY

Young people learn in spite of us, by chance or by intent. The teaching of values is the responsibility of all, at home, on the job, in the schools. We teach values primarily by providing guidelines, by example, and by demonstration. Since we are never sure who or when someone is observing us, we must do our best to be positive role models and to model *universal* values. We need to stress shared universal values, not our personal values or values that may alienate, divide, and separate.

9   —————————————————————————

Morals

To educate a person in mind and not in morals is to educate a menace to society. (Theodore Roosevelt, 1951)

Chapter 9 explores reasons why we believe and act as we do and examines the morals that guide our actions and influence our lives.

HOW MORAL ARE WE?

"Teach morals in my public school? Forget it. Morals are to be taught in the home and in churches and in synagogues. That is where moral education belongs. I won't have liberal teachers teaching morals to my children and grandchildren!"

Comments such as these are common today. They occur not only because there is a distrust of our educational system and a distrust of teachers and administrators but because there is such a wide difference in how parents and others interpret the implications of teaching morals.

Most people consider themselves moral. They do not question being moral; they just are. This is probably because concepts of morality are learned early in life from parents, grandparents, aunts, uncles, cousins, foster families, or even from those in authority at detention centers, jails, and other security institutions. Since family members provide food, shelter, and protection, few questions are asked by those being influenced. It is assumed family members are proper in their actions. Only later are their motives questioned.

Morals and morality have long been tied to formal religions. Some people behave and live in a "good" way so that after their death they will reap the benefits. According to their beliefs, if they have lived a good life, in the period following death they shall transcend this mortal state and go to a far better place, one where there will be no lack of water, no hunger, no cold, no sickness or disease, a place where all will live in peace and in comfort and will possess riches beyond imagination. There they will rejoin those who have passed on before. Or if persons belong to a caste system, as in Buddhism, according to their beliefs when they die, they will be reincarnated to a much better life if they have lived a "good" life, eventually to reach a state of bliss, known as nirvana, in their ultimate reincarnation.

Religion has a far-reaching effect on how we interpret our moral actions and how we respond when we find ourselves in situations that challenge our moral beliefs. Yet morals and morality are difficult to write about and discuss because people differ so in their beliefs, generally belonging to at least one of four groups.

First are those who equate morals and morality with religion. Members of this group assert that their own definitions of morals and morality are the *right* ones. They believe without question that they are right. Their verification of rightness is based upon divine guidance, duly recorded and interpreted by divinely inspired individuals. Their morality is based on faith.

The second group may look to science, to reason, or to what is best for the majority in society as determinants for moral decisions. These are the so-called rationalists.

The third group denies the need for any moral decisions. They do what is best for themselves as individuals without concern for the society of which they are a part.

The fourth group never questions whether something is moral or immoral. Members of this group are content with the way things are. Mostly they prefer not to become involved with moral decisions or controversy. They let others make decisions for them and then follow along.

MORALS AND MORALITY DEFINED

Morality and the study of morals is a branch of philosophy, as are ethics and values. Quite often there may be confusion as to how ethics, values, and morals differ from each other. As noted in the previous chapters on ethics and values, the terms *morality*, *ethics*, and *values* are used interchangeably by some authors or they are combined as moral values, ethical morals, moral ethics, ethical values, and so on, by others.

Much of the confusion surrounding defining *moral* is caused by how authors, philosophers, and teachers perceive and use the term. For instance, the word *moral* is frequently used as an equivalent for *right*. In *Death in the Afternoon*, Ernest Hemingway wrote, "What is moral is what you feel good after and immoral is what you feel bad after" (Hemingway, 1932, p. 4).

In one definition, *morality* is "a term that focuses on principle rules and ideas that are related to human relationships, to how we deal with each other and with the world" (Purpel, 1988, p. 66). Continuing, Purpel (1988) states, "Our moral heritage, in addition to a commitment to the sanctity of the individual, includes an intense concern for justice, equality, forgiveness, mercy and, most important, an aspiration for a community infused with love" (p. 71).

The selection of morals begins at birth and continues throughout life. As mentioned earlier, at an early age children learn which morals are accepted by others. They learn this by watching the moral or immoral behavior modeled in their environment. Stiles and Johnson (1977) stated:

Morality connotes conformity to the rules of "right conduct" of an established ethnic, racial, or cultural entity such as a family, community, bloodline, or religious denomination. Moral behavior is learned. Parents are the prime teachers. Community attitudes and expectations, at least in homogeneous groups, support parental training. Religious institutions offer formal instruction and develop pressures for conformity. Schools are expected to provide additional instruction and reinforcements for morality through the values endorsed, the behavior approved and rewarded . . . and the examples set by teachers and other educational leaders. (p. xii)

If children observe unacceptable behavior or even immoral behavior, they may consider it *acceptable* if it is modeled by someone they respect. As a result, conflict between different interpretations of morally acceptable behavior may arise. For example, most people would agree that the elderly should be respected and helped, that this would be the right thing to do. It is not moral to rob, assault, and steal from them. If children are raised without respect for the elderly, they see nothing wrong in taking from them whatever they want and in the process treating them with anger, rage, or indifference.

Morality, or the state of being moral, like the term *moral,* has a wide range of definitions. They extend from general conformity to the rules of right conduct to being an instrument (incorporated in laws) of society for the guidance of individuals. Morality is reasonably simple. It means to do good. When we delve into the reasons for doing good, morality becomes a more complex issue. For whom do we do good—for others or for ourselves? Morality promotes rational self-guidance and self-determination of its members.

Morality also has religious connotations because "morality includes insight and action—insight into the nature and likely consequences of behavior in order to recognize good and evil, and action to secure the good and diminish evil" (Wheelis, 1974, p. 6). Most countries have resisted a national code of morals, yet communist ideology incorporated such a code as part of its political credo. Richard DeGeorge (1969), in his book *Soviet Ethics and Morality*, listed the twelve principles that comprised "the moral code of the builder of communism."

The party holds that the *moral code of the builder of communism* should comprise the following principles:

1. devotion to the communist cause: love of the socialist motherland and of the other socialist countries;
2. conscientious labor for the good of society—he who does not work, neither shall he eat;
3. concern on the part of everyone for the preservation and growth of public wealth;
4. a high sense of public duty; intolerance of actions harmful to the public interest;
5. collectivism and comradely mutual assistance; one for all, all for one;
6. humane relations and mutual respect between individuals—man is to man a friend, comrade, and brother;
7. honesty and truthfulness, moral purity, modesty, and unpretentiousness in social and private life;
8. mutual respect in the family, and concern for the upbringing of children;
9. an uncompromising attitude to injustice, parasitism, dishonesty, careerism, and money-grubbing;
10. friendship and brotherhood among all peoples of the USSR; intolerance of national and racial hatred;
11. an uncompromising attitude to the enemies of communism, peace, and the freedom of nations;
12. fraternal solidarity with the working people of all countries, and with all peoples. (p. 83)

Were one to remove the political overtones, few would be critical of most of this "national" code of morality.

HISTORICAL DEVELOPMENT OF MORAL CONCEPTS

The historical development of morals and morality in the Western world can be divided chronologically into four time periods. They are the classical age, the medieval period, the Renaissance, and the modern era.

Classical Age

Being a good person and trying to live the "Good Life" was the goal of most who lived in the classical period, a period extending from the early Greek philosophers to the fall of Rome in A.D. 410.

Morality, like ethics and values, was a concept early Greek philosophers such as Socrates, Aristotle, and Plato discussed and debated. Then, as now, different views and opinions were expressed. Most early Greek philosophers felt that the highest goal was to live a good life. According to Kurtines and Gewirtz (1984): "Plato's conception of morality was idealistic. He sought the true form of the Good in an ideal world, the Platonic world of ideas, a world separate and remote from the everyday world of human experience" (p. 8). Aristotle's conception of morality, however, was more down to earth than Plato's. Kurtines and Gewirtz (1984) explain: "Humans are natural organisms, and morality is concerned with achieving the good life here and now. . . . It is the exercise of reason over appetitive and sensory desires. It is the life of right conduct—right conduct in relation to other persons and in relation to one's self" (p. 9).

Medieval Period

Beginning in A.D. 313 "the emperor Constantine granted liberty of worship to Christians, and in A.D. 325 the Council of Nicaea defined basic Christian doctrine, declaring all other interpretations heretical" (Albert, Denise, & Peterfreund, p. 106). "For 10 centuries, the intellectual history of the Western world evolved within a framework unified by a single great belief; the nearly universal acceptance of the truth of Christian revelation" (Kurtines & Gewirtz, 1984, p. 11). Thus,

medieval conceptions of morality . . . differed from classical conceptions in that they tended to be spiritual and other worldly rather than secular and this-worldly. The ancient and medieval world did, however, share one important belief—a belief in the existence of objective moral standards. The ancient Greeks sought the knowledge of objective standards through the use of reason, the faculty of the human mind capable of the apprehension of universals; the medieval mind sought the knowledge of objective moral standards through faith in the truth of divine revelation. (Kurtines & Gewirtz, 1984, p. 13)

Renaissance

With the end of the Middle Ages and the beginning of the Renaissance came a revival of learning in all fields, especially science, mathematics, art, music, and literature. It was a period of transition. The Catholic Church lost some of its domination in directing the lives and thoughts of people. People looked for answers and reasons why some things occurred as they did. Copernicus expressed opinions contrary to those of the established Church by stating the earth was round and rotated around the sun. Newton formulated the laws of gravity and Galileo used his refined telescope to look beyond the earth. If the Church could be wrong in such areas, was it possible it could err in others? The result was that many who disagreed with the Church edicts were either excommunicated or ordered to remain silent and to not challenge Church doctrine in the future. Thus, as Kurtines and Gewirtz (1984) observed, "by the end of [the] Renaissance reason had triumphed over faith" (p. 15). They continued by saying, "It was during this period that modern science firmly established for itself a central role in the mainstream of western thought, and it appeared to the Enlightenment thinker that man was on the verge of unlocking all of the secrets of the physical universe" (p. 16).

Modern Era

The development of modern moral thought and morality was spurred by a proliferation of publications by seventeenth-century philosophers. "In France and Britain, the centers of philosophical research in the seventeenth century, incomplete theories of morality abounded, as philosophers who stood by traditional Christianity, confronted with the radical unorthodoxies of Hobbes [the British philosopher] and Spinoza, upheld the rationality of the principles of Christian morals" (Donagan, 1977, p. 8).

In an age of great thinkers such as David Hume, Francis Hutcheson, Jean-Jacques Rousseau, and the Earl of Shaftsbury, Immanuel Kant (1724–1804) stood out as the first major philosopher to develop a complete philosophical theory of morality. Kant believed that morality is doing one's duty; that we should respect all human beings impartially and avoid exploiting anyone; and that the morally correct action is one done out of reverence for the law (Albert et al., 1953).

Another moral philosopher of the modern period was John Stuart Mill (1806–1873). He was a proponent of a moral theory known as utilitarianism. "This theory holds that one ought to do that which will provide the greatest benefit for society. . . . The key here is that utilitarianism is a moral theory which is committed to the position that the welfare of society is of paramount importance in assessing moral worth" (Ashmore & Starr, 1991, p. 30).

Friedrich Nietzsche (1844–1900), another philosopher during this modern period, proved to be a thorn in the side of other moral philosophers. He relentlessly attacked what he saw as the "decadence and hypocrisy of traditional European morality— a morality which will eventually lead to the eclipse of Western civilization" (Albert et al., 1953, p. 255). Many of the intellectuals of the period who supported him were also dismayed by the loss of individuality brought on by the machine age.

In the United States the concept of morality lagged behind the thinking and philosophy of Europeans such as Rousseau and others of his time. Early Americans who had the privilege of an European education were aware of the changes in philosophical concepts on the Continent.

Colonial views on education were shaped by the theological outlook of Calvinism in New England and by the Church of England in the South. . . . In addition to reading, writing, spelling and arithmetic, children in the colonial period were instructed in catechism. As the view of the child became more liberal and the interests of the people more secular, religious instruction gave way to moral instruction. (Tanner & Tanner, 1980, pp. 200–201)

MORALS, MORALITY, AND EDUCATION

The teaching of morals in public schools followed much the same path as the teaching of values. Stories and poems with strong moral implications were included in McGuffey Readers. Other than formal classes in philosophy at the high school and postsecondary levels, formal teaching of morals and morality was left to parents and religious institutions.

Richard McAdams (1993), in his book *Lessons from Abroad: How Other Countries Educate Their Children*, states:

The consensus on values that once made moral education part of the public school experience no longer exists. Court challenges have not only removed prayer from the schools, but have made schoolteachers and officials wary of making firm statements on any moral issue, for fear that they will be accused of manipulating the minds of their students. Never-the-less, educators see a critical need for moral instruction, a need that they attempt to meet through values clarification activities that satisfy no one, but anger and offend a vocal minority. (p. 321)

In the United States today, although not part of the formal curriculum, morals and morality still exist through the manner and style in which teachers explain issues, the examples they choose, the way they treat others, and their conscious and unconscious personal modeling. The inherent danger is that what they model and unconsciously teach will conflict with morals modeled by members of the student's family. This was never more true than during the Vietnam conflict. People questioned the morality of our involvement in Southeast Asia. The government, including the president (i.e., Dwight Eisenhower, John Kennedy, and Lyndon Johnson), attempted to justify our involvement on the basis that we, the United States, were trying to stem the tide of communism. Many, especially college students, did not accept this explanation and viewed the conflict as an immoral, illegal war.

A strong antiwar movement and protest, together with school desegregation and the elimination of prayer from the schools, had a direct effect on education. In addition, the drug culture expanded, love meant "never having to say you are sorry," and the sexual revolution intensified. Young people grew up wondering whom to believe—the president? Congress? Their parents? Teachers? The movies? Or the new rock musicians and their "Anything is okay" or "Just do it" philosophy?

The years following the Vietnam conflict reflected the lack of direction and confused state of education. SAT scores continued to decline and American schools dropped in international ranking. This was followed by a public outcry for accountability. The curriculum in most schools soon reflected the mood change, and a heavier emphasis was placed on mathematics, the hard sciences, computer skills, and foreign languages. A study of philosophy and morals education was noticeably absent even though this was not the case in foreign countries. For example: "Moral education is one of the compulsory subjects in Japanese schools at every grade level. One hour each week is devoted to development of ethical and moral reasoning so that students will be able to resolve moral dilemmas. The Japanese regard moral issues as essentially social or interpersonal problems, which cannot be resolved by strict rules or objective principles" (McAdams, 1993, p. 200).

Teachers in the schools today represent a wide range of educational, religious, ethnic, and social backgrounds. Most have no special training or basic education in teaching moral concepts, other than their own experience. Most would be reluctant to become involved in teaching morals because of the pressure that might be brought to bear by a vocal minority. Confirming this reluctance, Walter Feinberg, in his contribution to *The Moral Dimensions of Teaching*, writes:

We are witnessing a remarkable change in the circumstances of public school teaching. The moral foundations of compulsory education are being questioned as people of many different political and educational persuasions challenge its legitimacy. Alternative schools grow more popular, proposals for vouchers and tuition tax credits receive sympathetic hearings, home schooling appeals to more people, and the public schools' moral authority continues to diminish. Unless a new moral conception of public education is developed, public schools may stand as meaningless institutional shells, reminders of once larger purposes, and policy makers will have little guidance to help them evaluate the merits of many conflicting proposals for public education that have been offered in recent times. (Goodlad, Soder, & Sirotnik, 1990, p. 155)

Yet all teachers and administrators model behavior, express values, and behave in an ethical manner that models the moral philosophy each espouses.

Addressing teacher preparation institutions, John Goodlad et al. (1990) state: "Our society simply cannot afford teachers who fail to understand and assume the moral burden that goes with developing humane individuals within the context of a political democracy. Teacher preparing institutions share the moral burden" (p. 21). He continues by saying: "Opportunities to gain access to the most generally useful knowledge are maldistributed in most schools with poor and minority children and youth on the short end of the distribution. This is morally wrong, whatever the arguments regarding teachable classes, teacher comforts, parent preferences, and even achievement" (p. 22).

This idea is most clearly stated by William Bennett (1993) in *The Book of Virtues*:

Moral education—the training of the heart and mind toward the good—involves many things. It involves rules and precepts—the do's and don'ts of life with others—as well as explicit instruction, exhortation, and training. Moral education must provide training in good habits . . . and moral education must affirm the central importance of moral example. It has been said that there is nothing more influential, more determinant, in a child's life than the moral power of quiet example. For children to take morality seriously, they must be in the presence of adults who take morality seriously. And with their own eyes, they must see adults take morality seriously. (p. 9)

Teaching is a profession that involves much more than giving information to students. Those who teach are involved with students in many different ways. Teachers can pay strict attention to a single student or they can work with small or large groups. They can stop a fight, referee a ball game, divide the class into teams. More importantly, they can discuss a student's behavior, ability, or home atmosphere with other teachers. Teachers may not even be aware of the moral influence they have on their students *and* their coworkers. According to Barry Bull in his chapter in *The Moral Dimensions of Teaching*:

Teachers who understand their impact as moral educators take their manner quite seriously. They understand they cannot expect honesty without being honest or generosity without being generous or diligence without themselves being diligent. Just as we understand that teachers must engage in critical thinking with students if they expect students to think critically in their presence, they must exemplify moral principles and virtues in order to elicit them from students. Teachers must also draw attention to what they are doing and why. . . . There must also be support for those who try to model the teacher and some sense of safety for those who are not ready to do so. (Goodlad et al., 1990, p. 135)

MORAL SKEPTICISM

When a skeptic asks why we are moral, believe as we do, behave as we do, we probably answer with something like this: "We believe in morality because it is true. We believe it is wrong or immoral to commit certain acts such as murder or incest because it is wrong, inhumane." We usually haven't thought much about morality because that is how we are, how we have been raised by our parents, family, and community.

We haven't questioned our own moral beliefs because they work for us. As long as we live, work, and study where all tend to have the same moral beliefs, we experience few problems.

But suppose changes occur. Perhaps we take a new job, change schools, move into a new community or to a different country. If we continue to think as we have, we may discover problems or experience conflicts with our new peers, neighbors, and friends, even with the law (Wallace, 1994). After considering our position, we may remain steadfast in our moral convictions or may consider alternatives. Whichever we choose, options must be considered, choices made, and accountability for our actions accepted.

THE FUTURE

Some may claim that morality is a matter of choice, like the flavors of ice cream or breakfast cereals. Each person, some claim, is free to decide which morals, if any, should be honored and respected. Frederick Close (1993) chooses to differ with that approach.

As members of the moral community, we cannot allow Ted Bundy to murder young women even though it may be to his liking. We must not say of the Holocaust, "Well, the Nazis had their morality, we have ours, and who are we to judge them?" On the contrary, being moral means making such judgments. Being neutral about wanton killing is a moral failure. . . . The moral community cannot allow its members to kill, steal, etc. if they enjoy it because then the community and morality would cease to exist and everyone would be worse off. . . . Most young people gradually come to appreciate and accept the shared moral beliefs which every society must have in order to operate. (Close, 1993, p. 3)

Those who intend to teach young people have a difficult task. What used to be a typical family—mother, father, brother, sister, and perhaps a pet—seldom exists. In a society where *over* one-half of the marriages end in divorce, children all too often find themselves in a family situation with one resident parent, with a stepparent, with foster parents, or with parents *in loco parentis* (sheriff's ranches, juvenile homes, etc.). In such situations, which behavior to emulate and whom to follow can be very confusing. Unintentional modeling is always possible. Consider the effect of cheating on one's income tax form and bragging about it, or padding insurance claims. Or what about lying about the age of a child to get cheaper prices for meals, theater tickets, or transportation? Behaviors such as these, especially if undetected, declare that it is acceptable to compromise moral beliefs.

Moral decisions become more difficult when punishment for crimes enters the equation. For example, should young people be incarcerated with older people? Decisions become even more difficult when life-and-death issues are considered. Should people with incurable diseases be legally allowed to end their lives? Is it proper to end the lives of people who are brain dead? These are problems with strong moral implications.

Children are aware that all is not equal. In a keynote address given at the LBJ Library (September 26, 1992), Jonathan Kozol commented about the disparity of per-pupil funding between different school districts. He questioned the morality of spending $4,000 dollars per pupil in Camden, New Jersey, $8,000 per pupil in Princeton, New Jersey, and $16,000 per pupil in

Great Neck, Long Island, New York. Are there really $4,000, $8,000, and $16,000 babies? If so, what are the differences? Are some smarter, more attractive, better athletes, better babies?

Later Kozol visited a very affluent high school in Rye, New York, and spoke to an advanced placement history class, where he described the differences in equipment, resources, and especially facilities and maintenance between districts that spend $4,000 per pupil and districts that spend $16,000 per pupil. After explaining this, he asked if students thought that was fair. One student responded that it wasn't fair, that the game was rigged. Another said, "This is what it means to me. It means that for the rest of my life all my victories will be contaminated by the knowledge of injustice." Kozol decided to push further and asked, "What if we simply had a steep supplementary progressive federal income tax—maybe a 50 percent supplement for people who earn over $200,000 a year and earmark every bit of that for public education. What if we funded every child equitably in America except a little more for the kids who have the greatest need?" (Of course, most of their parents earned more than $200,000, or they couldn't afford to live in that area.) Finally, one young lady said, "I just don't understand how that would benefit me."

How does one deal with the morality of hunger, disease, capital punishment, abortion, and the homeless? Possibly these are the most immoral issues of our time. Maybe the moral questions to address are: Why are there homeless people? Why is there hunger when there are food surpluses elsewhere? Why does there have to be a law to make abortion legal or illegal? What is wrong with a society that believes it must use capital punishment to deter crime? Why do we permit people to continue in public office, at all levels, when they have betrayed public trust?

Have we given up expecting moral conduct that benefits others? Have we given up expecting moral conduct that makes society a better place?

CONCLUSION

The "What's in it for me?" philosophy makes a strong statement about the moral attitude of many in our country. It contradicts the basic premise of morality (to do good), and it contradicts being a positive and helpful member of a community.

One of the best rationales for being a moral person, one who models morality, comes from Kevin Possin and Craig Hanson (1993) of Winona State University in Minnesota. They use an article by Peter Singer in one of their student guides. Singer's (1972, Spring) article, entitled "Famine, Affluence, and Morality," builds a strong case for being a moral person and for acting in a moral way.

Singer (1972) first identifies a problem: People in a small foreign country were dying for a lack of food, shelter, and medical care. Then he points out that more affluent countries were doing little to alleviate the tragic situation.

If it is in our power to prevent something bad from happening, without thereby sacrificing anything of comparable moral importance, we ought, morally to do it. By "without sacrificing anything of comparable importance" I mean without causing anything else comparably bad to happen, or doing something that is wrong in itself, or failing to promote some moral good, comparable in significance to the bad thing that we can prevent. (p. 231)

Singer, of course, is suggesting that if it costs a person relatively nothing in regard to personal comfort or finance, why not make the decision in a moral fashion, a decision from which all would benefit?

SUMMARY

Morals is a branch of philosophy that focuses upon principles and ideas that guide our relationships with others in society. Morals are occasionally referred to as rules of good conduct or "doing the right thing." Morals are learned principles that begin to be formulated early in childhood. Morals and morality are usually deeply ingrained in one's personal philosophy but *can* be altered or changed. They are much more deeply seated than values, however. At a time when traditional family structure is changing and the teaching of morals is not accepted in public schools, educators are among the few in a position to provide positive modeling of socially acceptable morals.

Although moral training and morality is by many equated with organized religion, living a moral life and having a strong sense of morality can indeed stand alone, without any other justification than it supports and enhances the society in which we live.

RECOMMENDED READING

Many excellent resources are available for studying the topics of morals and morality. The following are four we found to be most helpful

Barlett, D., & Steel, J. (1992). *America: What Went Wrong?* Kansas City, MO: Andrews & McMeel.

Kurtines, W., & Gewirtz, J. (1984). *Morality, Moral Behavior, and Moral Development.* New York: Wiley.

Singer, P. (1973). *Philosophy and Public Affairs.* Princeton, NJ: Princeton University Press.

Stiles, L., & Johnson, B. (1977). *Morality Examined: Guidelines for Teachers.* Princeton, NJ: Princeton Book Company.

10

Indifference

Indifference, to me, is the epitome of evil. The opposite of life is not hate, it's indifference. The opposite of art is not ugliness, it's indifference. The opposite of faith is not hearsay, it's indifference. The opposite of life is not death, it's indifference. Because of indifference, one dies before one actually dies. (Wiesel, 1986, p. 68)

Indifference is a lack of feeling. It is being detached, unconcerned, and disinterested. It is being void of emotion, passion, and excitement. It is *turning inward*. It is worse than ignoring because ignoring recognizes another's existence. Indifferent persons do not care enough to not care.

INDIFFERENCE AT THE INTERNATIONAL LEVEL

When geographically removed from another country, it is comparatively easy to become indifferent to its problems. When one reads "20 Believed Killed by Landslide in Sri Lanka" (*The Free Press*, October 9, 1993), "Passenger Jet Shot Down; 28 Dead [Sukhumi, Georgia]" (*The Free Press,* September 22, 1993), "Tribal Guerrillas Gun Down 87 People [Manipur, India]" (*The Free Press*, September 16, 1993), "Quake Hits India, 50 Feared Dead [Maharashtra, India] (*The Free Press*, September 30, 1993), it is comfortable to say "that is so terrible," and then turn to the sports section.

Throughout the world there are catastrophes—earthquakes, floods, typhoons, tornadoes. An example is the cyclone that hit Bangladesh in 1991 and claimed more than 131,000 lives ("Cyclone warning system," 1994). After reading of such disasters some find it easy to rationalize: "My puny input will have little or no effect on a problem so large. If I contribute money, most will go to administrative costs such as high salaries and plush offices for the president of the organization. I could send food but that will end up on the black market. After all, I don't even know these people. I'll wait for something closer to home to support." Some justification for such thinking is real, however. For example, the television newsmagazine "Day One" recently "charged that because of excessive expenses, less than 3% of the $2.1 million raised by the Warwick Foundation reached the intended AIDS charities" (Scott, 1994, p. 2).

It is also easy to forget that those who survive disasters manage to exist with a lack of food, drinkable water, adequate housing, and limited finances. Aid is often slow in arriving and insufficient in quantity. Many people contribute immediately, then become involved with their own lives and problems. It does not take long for indifference to set in.

In 1994 a disaster of great magnitude occurred in Rwanda, Africa. "Up to 200,000 people are estimated to have been killed in little more than six weeks, most of them Tutsis hacked or clubbed to death by Hutu militiamen wielding machetes, clubs, spears and knives" (Mbitiru, 1994, p. 2A). Eventually over one quarter of a million citizens of Rwanda fled to four neighboring countries ("Refugees: Cholera feared," 1994). Before the killing was well underway, most foreigners fled; and since few suffered, Rwanda became for many Americans just a series of newspaper articles. Rwanda is an example of indifference at a gigantic level.

Using information provided from the "Bread For Life" organization, the *Leader*, a publication of the United Methodist Churches in Minnesota, reports that despite increased charitable efforts hunger is still climbing. They also report that although contributions to alleviate hunger worldwide have increased, the need for more aid has grown even faster. They note that worldwide 1.3 billion people live in absolute poverty and that 1.0 billion people subsist on less than one dollar a day ("Hunger still climbing," 1993, p. 11).

It is all too simple to send a donation after a catastrophe and forget that problems continue, even escalate. Fortunately, relief agencies such as the International Red Cross, the Salvation Army, and many church organizations do not act and then forget. Long after the disaster occurs, they continue providing food, clothing, and medicine, in addition to medical and administrative personnel.

INDIFFERENCE IN THE UNITED STATES

Those who are indifferent lack empathy, see the realities of life only through their own eyes, and consider only their own morals, values, and ethics.

In the United States corporate raiding is an example of total indifference to the needs of others. When a company is purchased for tax loss purposes, pension funds are removed, the company is allowed to go into bankruptcy and insolvency, and jobs are lost; this shows a total disrespect for and indifference toward the human beings whose lives are affected. It is far worse than "stealing cars and selling off the parts" (Dimma, 1991, p. 245).

Another example of corporate indifference is the following:

In February, Drexel Burnham Lambert went bankrupt. Just a few weeks earlier, they contrived to pay out $270 million in bonuses for 1989 performance. More or less simultaneously, 5000 of their white-collar people were thrown out of work. With Milken gone, the largest bonus, a paltry $107 million, went to Peter Ackerman. Leon Black went into a towering rage because he received only $12 million. His histrionic tizzy got him an additional $3 million.

So many dollars for so little benefit to society. (Dimma, 1991, p. 245)

In America there is indifference toward welfare and Aid to Dependent Children recipients, non-English-speaking people, immigrants and "boat people," the handicapped and elderly, the homeless, the unemployed; and there is indifference toward the human rights of persons of color.

For most of us, indifference is never thought of as such. People are so busy, so wrapped up in themselves, they seem to forget that others exist. Observe people walking along the sidewalk of a major city. They walk past the homeless and panhandlers, avoiding eye contact. Watch people as they pass patients released from mental hospitals or those who appear socially unacceptable. Observe the indifferent attitude, which speaks ever so loudly, that for all practical purposes street people do not exist.

Facts concerning something as basic as hunger in the United States are shocking. For example, in fiscal 1993, one of every six people in the United States participated in the U.S. Department of Agriculture federal food assistance programs, and whereas the median income of the richest one-fifth of U.S. income earners increased $3,500, more Americans (36.9 million) sank below the poverty level than at any time since 1962.

It is also a sobering statement about America's indifference when the facts are that "U.S. hunger can be eliminated by investing less than one percent of total federal spending—roughly 10 billion dollars—in existing Federal food programs" ("Hunger still climbing," 1993, p. 11).

Many are concerned about the funds that welfare families receive, but in reality much of the welfare problem is due to the absence of jobs paying more than minimum wages, accessible quality day care, and affordable health coverage for parents and their children.

Indifference is visible in nearly every neighborhood. Smokers are indifferent about who or how many are irritated by cigar or cigarette smoking. Others play music at a volume that occasionally reaches the threshold of pain. Still others mow their lawns early in the morning on weekends, when most would appreciate sleeping in late. Indifference is present when some choose to party until dawn, destroying the serenity of others.

Many are also indifferent to those who do not move rapidly—the handicapped using crutches or wheel chairs, the elderly. People in a hurry often push ahead, in the process making rude comments about those who retard their progress. If driving, they use their horn to express their displeasure, flash an uncomplimentary hand signal, or when passing cut in abruptly without signaling.

Often the indifferent become detached from their own indifference. Molly Ivins (1994) states it clearly: "Tolerance toward brutality grows gradually: Military torturers in Latin America who have been interviewed turn out not to be sadists but people who have gradually become indifferent to the pain of others" (p. 11).

What level of indifference toward feelings must an individual experience to set fire to the directory of the soldiers listed on the Vietnam Veterans Memorial in Washington, D.C. ("Vandals strike at," 1994, p. 3)?

INDIFFERENCE IN EDUCATION

Ask any group of teachers about indifference, and they can talk for hours. It touches them in many different ways. All have students who see no value in school.

For some children, indifference is a very powerful tool. It says, "Do whatever you want. Punish me, put me in 'in-school suspension.' Call my parents. Expel me. Flunk me. Keep me after school but you will only be punishing yourself." They are indifferent to the privilege of an education that has been provided for them.

Teachers who do not permit student indifference in language or behavior are becoming rare. However, one of the authors recently encountered one of those rare teachers. A young man refused to participate in physical education class and when encouraged to become involved in the activity called his teacher a "bitch." This very petite lady became anything but indifferent. She dragged him, protesting all the way, to the principal's office and made him call his mother and tell her what he had said. The student was very embarrassed and began to cry. One might correctly assume both his participation and language improved greatly since the incident.

How often is this same scenario carried out in other schools? As educators find themselves assuming more duties, responsibilities, required paperwork, and record keeping, it is inevitable some students will be short-changed in teacher attention, assistance, and counseling. Especially vulnerable are those students who are less aggressive; who lack language skills; and whose families teach them to avoid direct eye contact, accept without question, and not stand out in a crowd. Their behavior may be interpreted as indifferent; consequently, they may be treated with indifference.

Indifference can be observed at faculty meetings and at teacher curriculum writing workshops. Teachers may model indifference by gazing out the window during recitation or by clipping their fingernails or reading when a student is talking. Such behavior is not appropriate, if for no other reason than the disinterested message it sends.

There can be much indifference in testing, grading, and even in responding to the feelings of students. Too often teachers may be indifferent to the problems students have at home or with their friends. A teacher needs to model consideration and listen carefully for what is often unsaid.

Many times we comment on the indifference of young people. One has only to look around at our society and observe the forces that contribute to such an attitude. Indifference may develop from watching the questionable morals, values, and ethics of situation comedies or by viewing the violence so commonplace in the movies. Such violence and antisocial behaviors reflect an indifference for life. After being exposed to so much, it becomes commonplace, even easy, to be indifferent.

Maxine Greene (1978) writes in her book *Landscapes of Learning* that "the opposite of morality, it has often been said, is indifference—a lack of care, an absence of concern" (p. 43). Greene continues:

Moral education, it would seem, must be as specifically concerned with self-identification in a community as it is with judgments persons are equipped to make at different ages. It has as much to do with interest and action in concrete situations as it does with the course of moral reasoning. It has as much to do with consciousness and imagination as it does with principles. Since it cannot take place outside the vital contents of social life, troubling questions have to be confronted constantly. How can indifference be overcome. How can the influence of the media be contained. How can the young be guided to choose reflectively and compassionately even as they are set free. (pp. 47–48)

We adults may have contributed to an indifferent attitude toward suffering and violence by allowing television to be viewed even while dining. It is now possible to eat, carry on a conversation, and observe the carnage of warfare, fatal highway accidents, interviews at murder scenes, and violent crimes. By our actions as parents we signify that it is all right to be indifferent about such matters.

It is important for all to be recognized as worthy, contributing individuals. It is especially critical to remember this when dealing with young people. When we are indifferent to recognizing the existence of another human, especially a child, we fail to recognize the opportunity for positive impact. This is particularly true for family members.

Indifference retards, restricts, and inhibits the development of self-concept, dignity, and personal worth, especially in children, the ones who need it the most. Many parents inadvertently neglect their children in subtle ways, such as by allowing total freedom while growing up. Their children are not held responsible for their actions. They are allowed to be rude and indifferent to others in society.

As adults they neglect writing thank-you notes and send wedding invitations asking for cash so they won't have to exchange gifts. Probably these boorish young adults are unintentionally following behavior and values that were modeled for them.

SUMMARY

A powerful force, indifference affects people of all socioethnic status and educational backgrounds. As a potent force it often obscures personal and societal values, morals, and ethical training. Excuses and justifications for indifferent behavior result from selfishness and apathy toward the concerns of others.

After winning the Nobel Peace Prize, Elie Wiesel (1986) commented:

If there is one word that describes all the woes and threats that exist today, it's indifference. You see a tragedy on television for three minutes and then comes something else and something else. How many tragedies have we had recently? The Challenger, Chernobyl, the earthquake in El Salvador. And then there are the wars and those still in jail in the Communist countries. Because there are so many tragedies, a sense of helplessness sets in. People become numb. They become indifferent. (p. 68)

Indifference can become contagious. It can affect those unhappy in their job; those approaching retirement, seeking only to complete their work obligation; and the young who use it as power. Indifference can creep into our behavior and erode our guiding principles. Teachers must be aware of problems created by it, for awareness is the first step toward combating indifference.

Part Three
Education As a Source of Hope

11

Hope

> My theory has always been, that if we are to dream, the flatteries of
> hope are as cheap, and pleasanter than the gloom of despair. (Thomas
> Jefferson, 1817)

In a world filled with violence, greed, and intolerance, there *is* hope. This
chapter provides examples of hope, explains how education remains a
source of hope, and describes ways in which teachers can instill hope. We
believe President Clinton was correct when he said, "There is nothing
wrong with America that cannot be cured by what is right with America"
("Clinton inaugural," 1993).

EXAMPLES OF HOPE

Every day examples of hope appear in newspapers: A nine-year-old
takes charge when her mother and neighbor both give birth the same
morning ("Charmaine in charge," 1992). Deaf and mute high school students win the right to compete in the national Voice of Democracy speech
contest ("Teen girl who," 1992). Teenage mothers graduate from alternative
schools, turning away from welfare dependency (Goodwin, 1992). Traffic
deaths drop below 40,000 in 1992—the lowest annual figure in thirty years
("Traffic deaths apparently," 1992). The courts now address problems of the
homeless by dictating solutions such as setting aside "safe zones" for them
to "eat, sleep, bathe, cook, and defecate without fear of arrest" (Rohter, 1992,

p. 19A). Hundreds rally against racism and support families victimized by cross burnings ("Hundreds show support," 1992). Thousands march peacefully through Munich protesting intolerance, anti-Semitism, and rightist violence ("350,000 Germans march," 1992). American troops risk their lives in Somalia to feed the hungry ("Americans help restore," 1992). And there are no revolutions, riots, or violence when American presidential administrations change. These are examples of hope.

Personal examples of kindnesses that give us cause for hope also occur: someone holding open a door for us; someone helping us pick up the packages we drop when our hands are full; someone waiting at an intersection until we turn; a neighbor snowplowing our driveway; a phone caller saying "I'm sorry" when getting the wrong number. These are kindnesses we all experience at a personal level.

Yet other examples of hope surround us: The students of an elementary school principal who was bound, gagged, and robbed of school money raise $1,000 to replace it ("Dear Abby," 1992); high school students raise money for an eighty-year-old man who was hit over the head and robbed of $230 (J. Walsh, 1993); a man receiving $17,000 for a violin that cost $10 when he was in junior high shares this money with his parents ("Man sells violin," 1992); an usher at a horse-racing track finds a wallet with $1,800 and returns it to its owner ("Usher returns $1,800," 1991); police still stop traffic during funeral processions; seniors volunteer as foster grandparents for troubled youth; many kindnesses after hurricanes, floods, and other natural disasters are offered ("Nebraskans to send," 1992; "Troops carry food," 1992; "Donations help flood-ravaged," 1993); the Hospice Program and the Red Cross are still active; and self-help groups, such as Alcoholics Anonymous (AA), Overeaters Anonymous (OA), and Gamblers Anonymous (GA) help countless thousands each year. These are but a few of the kindnesses we witness every day. They give us hope for our world!

HOPE IN EDUCATION

To hope is natural. It is universal. Everyone hopes for something; indeed, it is safe to say that everybody is at all times hoping. What are your hopes—a better environment, the end to poverty, seeing your children graduate?

Education has and continues to be a source of hope for many because it serves as a vehicle for upward mobility. But today some people wonder if education still continues to be such a vehicle. Some say it does not because not *all* children have the opportunity to grow up to be president. The ladder of social mobility, they say, is not accessible to everyone (MacLeod, 1987).

It is easy for some to build a case for this belief. In their book *America: What Went Wrong?* Barlett and Steele (1992) state that 49 percent of those filing income tax returns in 1989 earned less than $20,000; the middle-class family's overall tax burden has risen to one-third of their income; and the government rule book, by which the economy operates, is rigged—by design and default—to favor the privileged, the powerful, and the influential. They add that social mobility during the 1980s was downward rather than upward and measured in terms of buying power; the wages of employees in manufacturing, retail trade, and service industry fell far short of the wages their parents and grandparents earned.

Every day we read and hear about such issues. The gap between the rich and the poor is well documented in the media: shrinking paychecks, disappearing factory jobs, fat salaries for corporate executives, and deteriorating standards of living.

Related elements of social inequality are identified in studies such as that by MacLeod (1987). He found the factors negatively affecting the aspirations of older boys within the same social class and school in a working-class neighborhood to be (1) living in public housing, (2) few years of formal schooling by parents and older siblings, (3) the sporadic employment record of family members, (4) the father's absence from the household, (5) the large size of families, and (6) family members' numerous encounters with the law.

Teachers, of course, have no control over these causes, but they indeed are and need to remain a source of hope. They must override depressed aspirations, focus upon helping children and youth personally discover hope, and help children see hope beyond present realities, to see they *can* graduate from high school, can turn away from welfare dependency, and can overcome inequities.

Teachers—a Source of Hope

Teachers serve as a source of hope in many ways. One teacher helped an adolescent overcome obesity and abusive alcoholic parents; the adolescent grew up to be a Minnesota Teacher of the Year. Another teacher helped several siblings in a Chicago family, living in a violent environment, with few successes and little hope, win certificates and ribbons for spelling, math, reading, and other academic achievements. These successes provided the family with incentives, nourishing their hope that at least the youngest child would graduate from high school and go on to college (Kotlowitz, 1990).

As a source of hope, teachers model discipline, helping students learn to think for themselves, changing the "won'ts" to "cans." Teachers are also a constant in students' lives. They give children second chances and believe in them when no one else does.

Teachers also serve as role models for encouragement. Did a teacher inspire you, help you through a difficult period in your life, lead you to new interests, give purpose and direction to your life? Generations are influenced by teachers who take the time to do more than just teach subject matter!

Teachers are exposed to real-life examples of hope every day. Here is one example from a student teacher, who writes: "I had one student who at the beginning of the semester was a troublemaker and never was really motivated to do anything. This past week he has been coming in for extra help, his notes are organized and highlighted, and he will even tell the class to shut up when they are loud. He is now one of my best students."

A second real-life example of hope comes from another student teacher, who writes: "Yesterday, Justin, an emotionally and behaviorally disturbed (EBD) student who has never taken out a piece of paper or pencil all year, wrote three-fourths of a page, Dr. Suess–style story during free-writing and asked to read it aloud to the class."

Teachers are surrounded by hope. It is this hope that encourages them to continue as America's best hope for helping students grasp the rungs of social mobility, for helping students learn to cooperate, communicate effectively, think critically, and value education and lifelong learning.

Instilling Hope

Teachers can instill hope in many ways. One way is to help students develop a positive self-concept. We all know this, of course, but sometimes we forget the simple yet important steps toward developing self-esteem: (1) providing opportunities for success, (2) creating nonthreatening classrooms, (3) using positive reinforcement, (4) holding students accountable, and (5) helping students set realistic goals, using appropriate methods to attain those goals. (Self-concept and goal setting is discussed in more detail in Chapter 13.)

Teachers cannot expect children to hope without some assurance that what is being hoped for will be attained. In 1915 Ladd cautioned that we cannot leave children to the depressing influences of dull and disappointing hopes. Hopes do not have to be extinguished so early in life. An Indiana middle school has a no-cut policy for extracurricular activities. "They have 120 track team members, 78 cross-country runners, 64 swimmers, a 66 member football team, and 73 cheerleaders. Students do not have to compete for a position or be devastated if they cannot make the squad" (Ryan, 1992, p. 10).

A second way teachers can instill hope is by teaching students to reject violence through nonviolent conflict resolution and peacemaking. This is so because we cannot hope for a more peaceful society and world if we do not teach methods for solving conflicts. They live in a society where a violent crime is committed every seventeen seconds; where the leading cause of injury among American women is being beaten by a man at home. where more than 100,000 weapons are brought into schools every day (McCarthy,

1992). Conflict resolution provides a source of hope for children because they learn how to manage conflicts other than through violence. They will less likely be beaten or shot if they try to resolve the conflict. The power of reversing the trend of violence toward one of peace rests in the hands of educators and parents (an issue addressed in Chapter 15).

A third way teachers can instill hope is to teach futurism. Learning about the future helps students realize there *is* a future. It gives them a sense of the interconnectedness between events and trends; it helps them anticipate present actions and future consequences; it gives them a perspective on reality; and it helps them acquire long-term outlooks. By holding present and future perspectives, students develop a sense of the future and become hopeful (Allain, 1992). Providing opportunities for students to think about what lies ahead also develops their creativity, imagination, critical thinking, and problem-solving skills. A simple exercise such as having students write about the future helps to develop these skills. The best part about an exercise like this is that students cannot be wrong!

A fourth way teachers can instill hope is by being in touch with reality and by holding students to realistic expectations. The first step is for teachers themselves to develop a broader vision of reality. Teachers need to understand that each person paints his or her own pictures of reality, so that our reality is not the same as that of others. Teachers need to under-stand how children and youth view the world. For example, how many teachers know what students experience outside the classroom—in the hallways, on the playground, and in locker rooms? In St. Paul, Minnesota, for example, two-thirds of junior and senior high school students say they have been threatened, robbed, or physically or sexually assaulted at school (Walsh, 1992, December 1).

When developing this vision of reality, teachers must recognize there is little chance for people to live worthily and well under any circumstances if they believe they are trapped and without hope (Ladd, 1915). Such people feel anger, alienation, hurt, and isolation (Boyd, 1992).

Children often feel cut off from hope. In their desperation some engage in deviant behavior, join gangs, murder their parents, commit suicide, and so on. Their sense of reality requires the perspective teachers can help develop. Obviously, children need much more than a new perspective, but this is a beginning. No matter how desperate children and youth may feel, teachers should provide opportunities for them to succeed, counsel them to remain human, to not give up on life, and to give hope a chance.

A fifth way educators can instill hope is by understanding the identities of their students. Teachers need to build bridges between the classroom culture and the culture of the home and community. "To educate their growing minority student population, teachers and administrators must find their methods in the homes and communities of their students" (Walsh, 1992, August 20, p. 5B). If there are no cultural bridges and if these two cultures are in conflict, students will have a difficult time learning (Walsh, 1992, August 20). According to MacLeod (1987), educators can no longer sing the familiar tune of "behave yourself, study hard, earn good grades, graduate with your class, go on to college, get a good job, and make a lot of money [because that] reinforces the feelings of personal failure and inadequacy working-class students are likely to hear as a matter of course. By shrouding class, race, and gender barriers to success, the achievement ideology promulgates a lie, one that some students come to recognize as such" (pp. 152–52). The truth is, however, "new research . . . estimates that, on average, each year of education, from grade school through graduate school, adds 16 percent to an individual's lifetime earnings" ("Brain trust: Study," 1992, p. 1A); and a "college diploma is worth $1,039 a month in extra pay" (Bovee, 1993, p. 2A).

Teachers need to convey these facts in ways that do not reinforce feelings of personal failure because attending college is *not* necessary for personal happiness and one can be quite successful without a college education. There is "new hope for kids who want other options" (Marshall, 1994, p. 58). Occupations with an anticipated growth in the next decade include "restaurant managers, credit clerks, transportation ticket agents, corrections officers, security guards, medical assistants, flight attendants, auto mechanics, computer repair technicians, electricians, dental assistants, and receptionists" (Marshall, 1994, p. 60). The military service is also a viable option for many. These occupations require apprenticeships, that is, on-the-job training as well as classroom education, but not necessarily college work.

Teachers can build cultural bridges that reinforce personal goals closely aligned with family and cultural expectations. By their own behavior teachers need to show they understand the realities of their students' lives. Those who work with a diverse group of students should (1) resist clinging to single-solution, essentialist positions; (2) eliminate condescension; (3) create an atmosphere in which all students can maintain self-respect, (4) explore class, race, and gender barriers; and (5) inculcate awareness of class, race, and gender stereotyping (MacLeod, 1987).

SUMMARY

Teachers must remain hopeful. There would be no other professions if there were no teachers. Educators are people of good will who realize that cooperation, compassion, and acceptance are tools for survival (Colson, 1992). Although the social and political realities of society seem harsh at times, and although teachers rarely get recognition for the seeds they plant, they do not need to look far for glimmers of hope.

As Jesse Jackson said at the National Democratic Convention in 1992, "Let's keep hope alive!" Hope is what our children need, what our teachers need, and what our nation and the world need. Teachers can make a difference in the lives of children and youth because teachers and education are and always will be some students' only hope. "Children must have at least one person who believes in them. It could be a counselor, a teacher, a preacher, a friend. It could be you" (Terry, 1993, p. 4).

12

Optimism versus Pessimism

The optimist proclaims that we live in the best of all possible worlds; and the pessimist fears this is true. (Cabell, *The Silver Stallion*)

We have all heard stories of the optimist viewing the vessel as half full and the pessimist viewing the vessel as half empty. In this chapter we examine the characteristics of optimism and pessimism and discuss the effects each has upon achievement.

OPTIMISM

Many equate hope with optimism, but it is one thing to be hopeful and another to be optimistic. Being hopeful and being optimistic are two different concepts. Being hopeful requires the ability to turn dreams into reality whereas optimism requires the resiliency to bounce back after disappointment (Seligman, 1992). These two concepts are closely linked, however. Acting in positive ways requires one to be optimistic, and accentuating the positive causes one to become hopeful.

Characteristics of Optimists

How do we recognize optimists? The research shows that optimists have many characteristics in common. For one thing, they engage in proactive activities; that is, they set goals, begin each day with a positive attitude, expand their interests and knowledge, find things to enjoy, make time for fun every day, and take control of their futures (McGinnis, 1990).

Optimists also have other characteristics in common. They do not take life too seriously, are sensitive to acts of generosity, recognize that others can be more talented than themselves, have strong passions and ambitions, bring out the best in others, do not harbor grudges, and are confident of their own achievements (McGinnis, 1990). Optimists do not, of course, always feel optimistic or express optimistic views. They, too, have negative feelings, yet at the same time they feel free to discuss them.

One can acquire a more optimistic outlook by employing strategies discussed in McGinnis's (1990) book *The Power of Optimism*. The main strategy he describes is designed to change one's intellectual habits by substituting positive thoughts for negative ones. Other selected strategies for helping one acquire the characteristics of optimists include looking for the good in bad situations, thinking of oneself as a problem solver, anticipating problems, keeping on trying, surrounding oneself with hopeful people, feeding one's spirituality, talking to a young person, getting to know someone new, laughing, enjoying celebrations even during difficult times, listening to uplifting music, and exercising.

Do Americans generally demonstrate the characteristics of an optimistic people, especially in light of being inundated with media reports about what has gone wrong with society? Or has daily exposure to headlines about violence, crime, greed, and poverty left many feeling pessimistic?

Recently a man complained to Bob Greene that he could not think of one good thing about our country. As a result of this complaint, columnist Greene invited his readers to send examples of good things about the United States. Here are a few of the over 50,000 items he received: "Travel from border to border, coast to coast with no visa, no permit, no questions, . . . American shoppers routinely buying a loaf of bread—without an eight-hour wait, . . . a baby duck hatching, . . . a bowl of popcorn, . . . the reassuring sound of the furnace kicking on in the middle of a tundra-cold night" (Greene, 1993, March 25, p. 5). These examples of what is good about America, as well as the fact that so many responded, indicate that the people of the United States are still optimistic. Perhaps their optimism is a remnant of the optimism our ancestors carried with them to the new world. Perhaps it is the optimism recent immigrants bring with them today: the belief they will be given a new opportunity—that our country can be a safe haven for refugees, those needing political asylum, or those escaping religious persecution.

How Optimism Affects Achievement

The traditional view of achievement is that success results from talent and desire. In his book *Learned Optimism*, Seligman (1990) suggests we reexamine this view. He believes those who fail, do so because optimism is missing, not because they lack talent or desire. After researching the concept of optimism for over twenty years, Seligman concludes that potential without optimism is meaningless. He believes that " 'talent' is vastly overrated. Not only is talent imperfectly measured, not only is it an imperfect predictor of success, but also the traditional wisdom is wrong. It leaves out a factor that can compensate for low scores or greatly diminish the accomplishments of highly talented people: [that is] explanatory style" (p. 154). By "explanatory style" he means that our accomplishments are in part affected by how we explain our success.

Explanatory style is very similar to attribution theory—the theory that people attribute their successes and failures to different causes. These causes can be considered permanent or temporary, universal or specific, and external or internal. The first and second parts of each pair of causes imply, respectively, pessimism or optimism. Whether you are an optimist or a pessimist stems from whether you think yourself valuable and deserving or worthless and hopeless (Seligman, 1990).

To increase achievement by using optimism requires more than saying positive statements to yourself. What you think about yourself when you fail is important. If your immediate thoughts are negative and destructive, if you blame yourself, you might have setbacks. The central skill of optimism is to change those negative thoughts to positive ones (Seligman, 1990). Seligman summarizes his theory this way:

It's a matter of *abc*: When we encounter adversity, we react by thinking about it. Our thoughts rapidly congeal into beliefs. These beliefs may become so habitual we don't even realize we have them unless we stop and focus on them. And they don't just sit there idly; they have consequences. The beliefs are the direct causes of what we feel and what we do next. They can spell the difference between dejection and giving up, on the one hand, and well-being and constructive action on the other. (1990, p. 211)

Seligman goes on to say that when we have pessimistic beliefs, we need to think of something else to distract ourselves. We also need to dispute these negative beliefs. Distraction alone will not have a lasting effect, but by giving pessimistic beliefs an argument, one can change from a reaction of dejection to one of exhilaration.

Optimism affects achievement at school, at work, and on the playing field. Optimism is a learned skill, one that can be permanently acquired, and one we can instill in children. Knowing this should motivate educators to help children and youth become more optimistic. They can do this by teaching children the skills of optimism as described above in the *abc* theory.

Educators can teach optimism in various other says. One way is to provide opportunities for success. When children and youth experience success, they believe in themselves—that they can achieve their potential—and they become hopeful. They see that their lives have purpose and meaning; they will not give in to failure, defeat, and helplessness.

A second way to increase achievement through optimism is by helping students learn to set goals. "Well-defined goals enable people to choose, design and implement their life and work objectives to achieve a mission or life purpose" (Rouillard, 1993, p. 78). Setting goals also helps individuals learn to become responsible for their own behavior. When people are in control of their own lives, they experience little or no desperation, become more optimistic about the future, and are more successful. Two helpful, easy-to-read, and inexpensive books about goal setting are Johnson and Johnson's (1986) *One Minute Teacher* and Rouillard's (1993) *Goals and Goal Setting*. (More information about goal setting is in Chapter 13.)

A third way educators can increase students' achievement through optimism is by promoting positive self-concept development. By increasing opportunities for success, children achieve more. As achievement increases, so does self-esteem. Teachers can explain to children that what they think changes how they feel; that by learning to identify bad thoughts, they can learn to change those thoughts into positive ones. A change in behavior leads to increased achievement and to thinking well of oneself.

PESSIMISM

Periods of pessimism can be traced throughout history. For example, nineteenth-century pessimism gave wide credence to the belief that there was a preponderance of evil over good in the world (Byron, 1965). The Victorian period of literature, poetry, and philosophy is laden with an undercurrent of pessimism. One example is found in the writings and poetry of James Thomson, which "were a contributing factor to the pessimism of his times as well as a result" (Byron, 1965, p. 163). Thomson's inability to foresee any good for the future of humankind was attributable to early religious doubts and fear of disbelief in the divinity of Christ and in immortality. These pessimistic feelings and attitudes had several effects on Thomson. He was unable to deal with his lover's death; he suffered from loneliness imposed by attacks of dipsomania, saw his life as futile, and desired annihilation (Byron, 1965).

Today people who carry pessimism to the extreme also have difficulty in accepting what life has dealt them. They, like Thomson, become depressed and suicidal. Pessimistic feelings and despairing attitudes have the same negative effect on well-being today as at any time in history.

Characteristics of Pessimists

How do we recognize pessimists? First of all, it is important to understand that having pessimistic feelings is at times normal behavior for everyone. However, research tells us that those inclined to think pessimistically more often than most people tend to have some of the following characteristics: They are depressed; feel worried and anxious; fail more frequently even when success is attainable; have poor physical health; have less zest for living; and are defeated when running for a high position, for example, politicians who campaign with a negative platform depicting everything that is wrong with government, business, and education (Seligman, 1990). These are the characteristics teachers might look for in students who may have pessimistic attitudes.

An interesting observation made by Seligman (1990) about one characteristic of pessimists is that they may be wiser than optimists. In making his case, he refers to Lionel Tiger's *Optimism: The Biology of Hope* in which Tiger argues: "The human species has been selected by evolution because of its optimistic illusions about reality. The capacity to act on the hope that reality will turn out better than it usually does is behind such courageous, or foolhardy, behavior" (Seligman, 1990, p. 108).

To further make his point, Seligman reasons that pessimists "accurately judge how much control they have [whereas] optimists . . . believe they have much more control over things than they actually do" (p. 109). "Optimists tend to distort reality in a self-serving direction while pessimists tend to see reality for what it is" (p. 111). This phenomenon, the "clash between reality and hope neatly illustrates the dilemma of illusory optimism" (Myers, 1992, p. 118).

How Pessimism Affects Achievement

Pessimism affects achievement through failure, defeat, and depression. Opportunities for failure abound in the classroom: not passing exams or consistently scoring low on all assignments; being told that one is not working up to potential; being assigned to the low reading or math group; not being called upon during class discussions; being afraid to give an answer for fear it may be wrong; always being the last one chosen on a team; and on and on.

Failure takes a toll on one's self-esteem. After a while children and youth may feel helpless because nothing they try seems to work. They may feel that attempts to improve their actions will be undermined. They give up, become defeated, and sense the futility. Positive thoughts are quickly turned into negative ones. For some, helplessness turns to hopelessness because after major defeats they may never try again.

Defeatist and pessimistic views and attitudes negatively affect achievement. Pessimists attribute life events to permanent, universal, and external factors. This way of thinking results in people always blaming themselves for negative events and consequences that they experience, rather than blaming others, things, or events over which they have no control. As a result, their self-esteem, and hence achievement, diminishes.

Pessimism also affects achievement through depression. Normal depression is common. However, "severe depression is ten times more prevalent today than it was fifty years ago. It assaults women twice as often as men, and it now strikes a full decade earlier in life on average than it did a generation ago" (Seligman, 1990, p. 10). Depression may be caused by defeat, failure, loss, and the belief that any actions are futile. To detect depression in students, look for these symptoms: negative changes in thought, mood, behavior, and physical response. These symptoms do not all need to be present, however, for one to be depressed (Seligman, 1990).

Many cognitive therapists believe that how we feel is determined by what we think. By changing habits of thought, one can turn pessimistic thinking (and depression) into optimistic thinking. These habits of thought are similar to Seligman's (1990) *abc* theory described earlier. The therapists suggest using five tactics for changing thought patterns. They advise (1) recognizing and identifying thoughts at the times one feels worst, (2) disputing those thoughts by presenting contradictory evidence, (3) re-attributing explanations and using them to dispute negative thoughts, (4) providing distractions from depressing thoughts, and (5) recognizing and questioning depression-ridden assumptions that rule what one does.

Anyone desiring more information about depression may find the book *You Are Not Alone* helpful. "Step by step [it] . . . leads depressed people to the realization that they are not isolated, they are not hopeless and help is available if they would but seek it" (Landers, 1993, p. 3E).

The role of educators in the classroom should be one of proactivity; they need to teach the skills of optimism so that common depression does not lead to severe depression or have a chance of consuming children's lives and affecting their achievement in and out of the classroom.

CONCLUSION

By assuming a role of proactivity, educators can help children and youth get on the road to well-being by teaching them a non-negative approach to thinking. But, says Myers (1992), non-negative thinking alone will not do the job. He believes that "the recipe for well-being [is] . . . a mix of ample optimism to provide hope, a dash of pessimism to prevent complacency, and enough realism to discriminate those things we can control from those we cannot" (p. 119).

Educators must continue to urge the nation to make education a priority. Without it, hope will be lessened by more pessimistic thinking. As adults we must wrestle with our own pessimism and work toward building a hopeful environment. In supporting this point Botstein (1993) suggests: "Education must be at the center of the future of America. The sooner this Administration comes up with a serious national education policy, the better off our children will be. We must learn to hope for them and cease crushing themwith our own ill-earned pessimism"(p. 40). Students *are* America's hope.

SUMMARY

Optimistic feelings, attitudes, and thinking lead to a healthy self-esteem and greater achievement. Pessimistic feelings, attitudes, and thinking lead to failure, defeat, and depression.

Since optimism is a skill that can be learned, educators can help students change pessimistic feelings and attitudes into optimistic, positive ways of thinking and behaving.

13

Self-Concept: Creating Your Own Rainbows

If there is one truth in the human heart, it would be to believe in itself, believe in its capacity to aspire, to be better than it is, might be. That it does exist in all people. (Faulkner, 1959, p. 78)

Erma Bombeck once wrote about the high school teacher who encouraged her to become a writer. This teacher impressed upon Erma the important details of writing etiquette, of course, but more significantly, from her point of view, did that which changed Erma's life—he pointed out destinations of dreams and offered suggestions on how to get there.

We can all recall similar examples of people who have influenced us. In his Pulitzer Prize–winning book *Truman*, McCullough (1992) writes that Harry S. Truman once said "the influence of his teachers on his life . . . was second only to that of his mother" (p. 59).

More real to life than not, in the television soap opera "As the World Turns," Lucinda Walsh, the long-lost older sister, asked her newly found brother how both he and their younger sister became so successful as adults when they had grown up with verbally and physically abusive parents. The brother answered, "Teachers helped us . . . a very special teacher took Neil under her wings and nourished her until I could."

Teachers help us to understand our potential and our aspirations. They believe in us, guide us, show us unlimited paths. They do not give us cut flowers, but teach us how to grow our own.

Teachers must never forget how much they influence their students. Teachers *are* rainbow makers. They *are* enhancers of self-concepts. The most important part of their job is to help children develop positive self-esteem. Their secondary task is to teach subject matter.

This chapter focuses upon how a positive self-concept leads to achieving goals, dreams, and rainbows.

SELF-CONCEPT DEFINED

Let us begin by defining *self-concept* and summarizing what the research reveals. This will provide a perspective for the reader to better understand what it takes to create rainbows. For our purposes, *self-concept* is broadly defined as a "person's total appraisal of his [or her] appearance, background and origins, abilities and resources, attitudes and feelings which culminate as a directing force in behavior" (LaBenne & Greene, 1969, p. 10). This all-encompassing definition supports what the research tells us about how we feel about ourselves and the impact of relationships upon us.

WHAT RESEARCH REVEALS ABOUT THE SELF-CONCEPT

Research reveals many conclusions about the self-concept. Some people may even regard these conclusions as maxims. Consider these few:

- A direct relationship exists between one's self-concept and one's behavior, perceptions, and academic performance.
- Self-concepts are influenced by those who administer rewards and punishments.
- Social class, family structure, parental behavior, ethnic background, religion, and the language spoken in the home affect one's self-concept and one's relationships with peers.
- Challenging experiences that maximize opportunities for success aid in the development of positive self-concepts.
- Self-concepts are not unalterably fixed but are modified by every life experience.

Teachers need to keep these maxims in mind when creating rainbows (dreams) for themselves and while guiding students toward creating their own.

Additional information helpful in developing a positive self-concept includes knowing that

- insecure people put others down so that they may re-establish their own self-worth.
- 85 percent of Americans believe a good self-image is very important.
- "happy people enjoy high self-esteem, a sense of personal control, an optimistic disposition, and outgoing personalities." (Myers, 1992, p. 119)

A useful book for gaining a better understanding of oneself is David L. Silvernail's (1985) *Developing Positive Student Self-Concept*. It is a brief and concise review of research on self-concept development. He describes several tests, scales, and inventories that can be used by you and your students.

HAPPINESS AND YOUR SELF-CONCEPT

What makes people happy can affect how they feel about themselves and can affect whether they will create rainbows for themselves and others. Therefore, it is propitious to briefly discuss the concept of happiness.

Everyone has his or her own definition of happiness. To some, it results from achieving goals (Rosemond, 1993). To others, happiness results from storybook makings. In comparing and contrasting the truer conception and the storybook version, Gardner (1963) states: "Storybook happiness involves a bland idleness; the truer conception involves seeking and purposeful effort. Storybook happiness involves every form of pleasant thumb-twiddling; true happiness involves the full use of one's power and talents. Both conceptions of happiness involve love, but the storybook version puts greater emphasis on being loved, the truer version more emphasis on the capacity to give love" (p. 121). In using the truer version to answer the question "What makes us happy?" perhaps, we also have to ask the age-old question posed by Jung: "In what way(s) is one's life meaningful?"

Implicit in the definition of happiness is its elusiveness. A Gary Larson (1993) *Far Side* cartoon recently showed a man carrying a box leaving a "Happiness" store. The caption said, "His few friends had told him he could never buy it, but Mr. Crawley surmised that they just didn't know where the store was" (p. 2). We all know, of course, that happiness is not so easily found as in a store.

The elusiveness of happiness is clearly and succinctly described below in a poem by Priscilla Leonard titled *Happiness*.

> Happiness is like a crystal,
> Fair and exquisite and clear,
> Broken in a million pieces,
> Shattered, scattered far and near.
> Now and then along life's pathway,
> Lo! some shining fragments fall;
> But there are so many pieces
> No one ever finds them all.
> You may find a bit of beauty,
> Or an honest share of wealth,
> While another just beside you
> Gathers honor, love or health.

Vain to choose or grasp unduly,
Broken is the perfect ball;
And there are so many pieces
No one ever finds them all.
Yet the wise as on they journey
Treasure every fragment clear,
Fit them as they may together,
Imaging the shattered sphere,
Learning ever to be thankful,
Though their share of it is small;
For it has so many pieces
No one ever finds them all.

As Leonard's poem suggests, happiness is elusive and is probably never experienced in the same way twice by the same person. It will probably also be defined differently throughout one's lifetime.

Happiness has different meanings for each of us. Tolstoy (1869) writes in *Anna Karenina* that "happiness rests only on oneself." Myers (1992) writes in *The Pursuit of Happiness* that the terms *happiness, life satisfaction,* and *well-being* are synonymous. Empirical and representative survey research on what constitutes happiness, he states, illustrate the differences between happy and unhappy people.

Happy people, he found, are energetic, decisive, flexible, creative, hope-filled, and sociable. They are also more trusting, loving, responsive, lenient, and forgiving than unhappy people. Happy people are less likely to be abusive and less likely to exaggerate slight criticism. They also tolerate more frustration, like themselves, believe they choose their destinies, spend more time looking at the brighter side, and are more willing to help those in need.

In contrast, Myers found that unhappy people are no joy to be around, brooding, distressed, depressed or bereaved, socially withdrawn, more vulnerable to illness, and hostile.

Happiness and positive self-concept development go hand in hand. One builds upon the other. People with a happy outlook on life, those who feel good about themselves, will reach for their dreams or rainbows.

TEACHERS CREATING THEIR OWN RAINBOWS

Earlier we stated that what makes people happy can affect their self-concept; this, in turn, affects how they create rainbows. But what is a rainbow? The word conjures up a mental image of an arc composed of the colors of the spectrum. For our purposes, though, rainbows are our dreams come true. People with positive self-concepts set goals that lead to attaining dreams or rainbows—and as the song in *South Pacific* says, "You got to have a dream. If you don't have a dream, how you gonna make a dream come true?"

Teachers sometimes forget or don't take the time to set new goals for themselves because it is easy to get caught up in the everyday affairs of the classroom. There are, however, some things teachers can do to create their own rainbows. They can examine their own attitudes, perceptions, needs, and expectations. Doing this helps them set new personal and professional goals. Teachers engage in self-renewal for themselves and serve as role models in the process.

Examining Attitudes, Perceptions, Needs, and Expectations

In creating rainbows it is helpful to examine our attitudes, perceptions, needs, and expectations. Examination and self-assessment of these areas helps us set personal and professional goals.

Attitudes

How do people determine their present attitudes? One way is to ask relevant questions: Am I optimistic or pessimistic? Am I happy or sad? Am I mellow or frustrated? What are my biases, predilections, and prejudices? Candid answers to these questions reveal one's present attitude(s). Attitudes reflect a person's disposition. If your attitude reflects the negative component of any of the questions above, ask yourself what you are going to do to change it.

Perceptions

Perceptions are an awareness of both self and others. How do you perceive yourself? How do others perceive you? Understanding how others perceive you, provides insight. This insight is referred to as the "looking-glass self" definition of self-concept because we perceive ourselves as reflected in a mirror. An operational definition of the "looking-glass self" by Vaughan (1988) explains this idea. She states: "As we look into the eyes of others, we may extend our outlook so that they may mirror back those beliefs to us. As we extend joy, love, commitment, devotion to our personal beliefs, so may others accept those ideas and mirror them back. As we extend enthusiasm, joy, and happiness, so do we receive and extend those messages. We have the power to influence others through our present actions" (p. 3).

Perceptions of self are affected by conformity and individuality. Developing and maintaining individuality is not always easy in a society that seemingly promotes conformity (e.g., eating a Big Mac in Iowa is the same as eating one in New York City or Moscow, and watching the same television programs is a coast-to-coast occurrence with reruns broadcast worldwide in different languages). When individuality is not stressed, one's self-concept becomes jeopardized. Moustakas (1967) describes how conformity affects one's identity:

When the individual is conforming, following, imitating, being like others, he moves increasingly in the direction of self-alienation. Such a person fears standing out or being different. He does not think through his experience to find value or meaning, does not permit himself to follow his own perceptions to some natural conclusion. He avoids directly facing disputes and becomes anxious in situations which require self-awareness and self-discovery. He becomes increasingly similar until his every act erases his real identity and beclouds his uniqueness. (p. 35)

One's understanding of self is crucial to developing and maintaining individuality.

Needs

Before setting personal and professional goals one must also examine one's needs. This is important to do because a functional and positive self-concept is affected by the fulfillment of one's needs. This leads to increased chances of creating rainbows. According to Abraham Maslow's hierarchy of needs, all of us have physiological needs, such as the requirement for food, drink, sex, and shelter; safety needs, such as the requirement for security, order, protection, and family stability; love needs, such as the need for affection, group affiliation, and personal acceptance; esteem needs, such as the desire for self-respect, prestige, reputation, and social status; and self-actualization needs, such as the need to find self-fulfillment and achieve personal goals, ambitions, and talent (Sprinthall & Sprinthall, 1990, p. 524).

When assessing needs, ask yourself these questions: What do I want (more or less power, love, freedom, fun, etc.)? What am I doing to get what I want? Is what I am doing working? If it isn't working, what will I do next? For example, if you determine you need more freedom in your life, you will also need to determine alternative means to accomplish this freedom, perhaps through your job or through your personal life. Perhaps your work schedule can be altered to set hours conducive to your peak productivity. If that is not possible, you might arrange to have one evening out each week to be with the girls (or boys), to shop, bowl, visit a museum, see a movie, and so on.

The power, love, freedom, and fun needs are important ones to assess in the goal-setting process. They are important because they affect us daily in either very positive or very negative ways. When these needs are being met, we feel good about ourselves and our achievements. When these needs are not met, we become frustrated and achieve less.

Expectations

Another area to examine before setting goals is that of your expectations as they relate to your personal and professional lives. Expectations are those things to which we look forward. They give us a prospect of the future—of what might be, could be. Setting expectations should be done realistically. Unrealistic expectations usually remain unfulfilled and lead to disappointment.

Finally, in assessing your attitudes, perceptions, needs, and expectations, consider the maxims listed below, which may improve your outlook.

- Learn to like yourself [by doing your best].
- Take control of your destiny [by setting goals].
- Practice expecting the best.
- Become more extroverted.
- Try acting happy.
- Consider new work.
- Sleep, sleep, sleep.
- Foster close relationships.
- Tie the knot.
- Have faith. (Thomas, 1993, pp. 66–68)

This advice may complement your pursuit of rainbows.

Setting Personal and Professional Goals

Rudolph Dreikers (1968) has said that in order to change what we are doing, we have to change our goals. After examining and assessing your attitudes, perceptions, needs, and expectations (as described above), construct a plan that includes short-range goals as well as long-range goals for your personal and professional development. These goals will bring you closer to achieving your dreams or rainbows.

Developing a plan with short- and long-range goals requires several steps.

First, develop a list of goals or competencies you expect to achieve during the next day, week, month, twelve months, five years, and ten years.

Second, prioritize these goals within each time period. Each short- or long-term goal will depend upon factors such as financial resources and feasibility. For example, a five-year goal might be to complete a master's degree. To reach that rainbow, smaller goals will have to be set—taking the Graduate Record Exam (GRE), applying to a graduate program, saving money to pay tuition, allocating time during the school year and during summers to take the courses, and so on.

Third, design a list of experiences that will help you attain these goals. In the example above, some of the smaller goals *are* the experiences that will help you attain your five-year goal. But if you set a goal of giving clear directions to your students, an experience you might design to achieve that goal would be to tape yourself on an audiocassette recorder and critique it after class.

Fourth, formally or informally select an advisory committee. It does not matter how you choose to do this as long as it is a comfortable process. Many people, including friends, colleagues, mentors, and spouses, may serve as advisors. Your goal should be to select trustworthy people who will provide feedback.

You and members of the advisory committee can establish criteria to assess whether you have achieved your goals as outlined on your personal and professional development plan. For example, you and the committee can establish periodic reviews for assessing your progress. As a part of the assessment, procedures might be recommended for facilitating, enhancing, and attaining your goals, dreams, and rainbows.

This self-renewal process will recharge your enthusiasm, creativity, and zest for living. For many people the attainment of a goal, no matter how small, leads to creating more goals. There is nothing like the positive feeling of a burst of renewed energy from the accomplishment of a task well done.

Before setting personal goals, consider reading two recently published books. The first, *The Seven Habits of Highly Effective People* by Stephen Covey (1990), suggests employing seven practices for creating personal change: be proactive; begin with the end in mind; put first things first; think win/win; seek first to understand, then to be understood; synergize, or work together; and engage in physical, mental, social/emotional, and spiritual self-renewal.

The second self-help book to read before setting personal goals is Gloria Steinem's (1993) *Revolution from Within: A Book of Self-Esteem.* It is intended for women, men, and children. Although research supports the idea that one's core self-concept is formed early in life, Steinem explains how you can unlearn and relearn ideas and experiences that perhaps have negatively affected your self-concept. This book, as well as Covey's, will provide you with a renewed understanding of yourself, as well as help you define some possible goals you may wish to achieve.

In setting new personal goals consider those that will help you grow, will make you feel better about yourself, and will improve the quality of your life. Infuse into all aspects of your life activities purposely created with your goals for improvement in mind. Such activities may include clearing credit card debts, engaging in home improvement projects, planning and taking vacations, losing weight, or learning to play a new musical instrument.

Strategies for Self-Renewal in the Classroom

There are several strategies that teachers can use for self-renewal in the classroom. These strategies also effectively enhance self-concepts. One strategy is to use observation and self-reporting as methods in diagnosing self-concepts. Ask yourself the following six questions:

Do I make my own decisions?

Do I feel secure with myself?

Do I have a positive attitude toward [teaching]?

Do I accept my race and ethnicity?

Am I able to deal with my inner conflicts?

Do I exhibit goal-oriented behavior? (Silvernail, 1985)

A second strategy for self-renewal is to examine the relationship between your self-esteem and your success as a teacher. There is a direct relationship between achievement and self-concept, with some research supporting the claim that improvements in achievement lead to more positive self-concepts (Silvernail, 1985). Ask yourself what you can do to be more successful in the classroom. Some questions teachers can periodically ask themselves as they reflect upon how to help students develop positive self-esteem are these:

- Do I encourage students to express their opinions and ideas?
- Do I convey to students my concern and interest for their needs?
- Do I exhibit a "businesslike and systematic" approach to the learning tasks?
- Do I exhibit enthusiasm for the learning tasks and in my classroom interactions?
- Do I interject humor into the classroom?
- Do I make a concerted effort to interact with all of my students?
- Do I encourage my students to praise their peers?
- Do I set realistic and challenging expectations for my students? (Silvernail, 1985, p. 48)

By engaging in the affirmative to these questions, teachers are more successful in helping children and youth develop healthy self-concepts. Successful teachers enhance their own self-esteem and experience greater achievements as educators.

A third strategy for self-renewal is to reinforce and praise yourself. People with high self-concepts tend to make positive statements to themselves after performing tasks (Silvernail, 1985). For example, one might say, "I am proud of myself for doing so well on the math test—I studied hard, and I feel good about myself." Praising oneself for a job well done is a major point in Johnson and Johnson's sequence of steps for goal attainment as described in their book *The One Minute Teacher* (1986).

A fourth strategy for self-renewal is to videotape yourself. Videotaping has many advantages. It gives immediate feedback about such things as your own use of praise, variety of questions asked, clarity of directions, elicitation of class participation, classroom climate, and so on. The accessibility to camcorders and VCRs makes this an easy process today (Anderson et al., 1992).

And fifth, a strategy for self-renewal in the classroom is to improve your self-concept through peer coaching. Viewing peers can be a learning opportunity. An interesting study using videotaping showed there were greater gains leading to positive changes in self-concept by those participants who were not videotaped themselves but who participated in the viewing and analysis of peers (Silvernail, 1985).

In summary, reevaluate yourself periodically through a self-designed, self-renewal process. This can be done by reassessing your attitudes, perceptions, needs, and expectations; setting realistic goals; developing a plan of action; and soliciting feedback from advisory committee members. Remember, the ultimate goals are to gain greater self-confidence in your ability, make your rainbows (dreams) come true, and serve as role models in the process.

GUIDING STUDENTS TOWARD CREATING
THEIR OWN RAINBOWS

Children who take responsibility for setting their own goals will be happy (Rosemond, 1993; Johnson & Johnson, 1986). But they also need to be taught that "no goal in life worth reaching for is achieved without a struggle. Setting goals means accepting and learning to deal with anxiety, frustration, disappointment, even failure" (Rosemond, 1993, p. 44).

Teachers know the pot of gold at the end of the rainbow is illusive. They must be willing and know how to show students that creating a rainbow for oneself, that is, setting goals, striving, anticipating, and initial achievement of the goal itself can be exhilarating, thrilling, and satisfying.

In guiding and supporting the self-development of students, educators need to help remove obstacles to individual fulfillment (Gardner, 1963). The most important obstacle to remove is the *fear of failure* because in order to grow, one must risk failure. But for some, failure without growth has become an everyday occurrence in the classroom. Continuous failure and defeat lead to pessimistic attitudes that can lead to depression. Some reasons for failure include (1) weak basic skills, (2) lack of confidence, (3) lack of motivation, and (4) frustration with school. The scariest thing for any child is to feel out of control without any choices (Santoli, 1993). "People who have little control experience lowered morale, more stress, and more health problems" (Myers, 1992, p. 114).

By creating a positive classroom climate conducive to risk taking, growth, and choice, teachers can help children overcome their fear of failure. Such environments encourage students to learn from their mistakes without being penalized and doomed to failure. Providing students with acceptance, approval, and sincere praise, even for minor accomplishments, helps children develop into healthy adults. Keep in mind that "children who grow up without warmth and praise become angry, critical adults" (Johnson & Johnson, 1986, p. 91).

Second, in guiding students toward creating their own rainbows, educators need to remove another obstacle to individual fulfillment—lack of love. As Fred Rogers of "Mister Rogers" said in an interview, "Everybody longs to be loved. And the greatest thing we can do is let somebody know that they are loved and capable of loving" (Santoli, 1993, p. 4). There will always be children who do not get the love and support at home they so desperately need. Teachers can help fill this gap by demonstrating genuine concern. Teachers do this everyday in classrooms across the nation—by taking the time to bolster the self-concept of a seventh-grader who is emotionally abused; by keeping personal toiletries, such as toothpaste and combs, and donated clothing for homeless children; and by supplying a coat for a first-grader who comes to school without one in subzero weather.

Third, in guiding children toward creating their own rainbows, educators need to help remove yet another obstacle to individual fulfillment— lack of motivation. Each person "should be doing something about which he [or she] cares deeply . . . and . . . it must be something not essentially egocentric in nature" (Gardner, 1963, p. 19). The more self-motivated one is, the greater the possibility for fulfilling one's potential (Johnson & Johnson, 1986).

Students have a basic motivational drive to improve, to learn, and to excel. But life is not perfect. Social, emotional, and environmental hurdles need to be overcome. Teachers and parents can help children regain their self-motivation. For example, a contemporary illustration is the story of two African-American boys growing up in the Henry Horner Homes in Chicago. This is described in Kotlowitz's (1990) book *There Are No Children Here* (this story was aired in 1993 as a made-for-television movie starring Oprah Winfrey). In spite of living in a violent neighborhood, in a bullet-ridden run-down apartment, with an extended dysfunctional family, Pharaoh, a nine-year-old, never gives up. After losing in a spelling bee one year, he is determined to do better the next—and he does by taking second place. His resiliency is astounding! More importantly, he has a dream to do something meaningful with his life—he wants to help make society a safer place to live. Again, teachers and parents can create a climate for motivating children by capitalizing on this basic motivational drive to improve, learn, and excel.

Getting children to do anything, let alone something for someone else, can at times be quite a challenge! This "something" could be tutoring peers, raising money for a charity, shoveling an elderly neighbor's sidewalk, or taking care of their siblings. Research shows that young people will be motivated to help others and act responsibly toward them only if they first learn to be responsible for themselves (Johnson & Johnson, 1986). Thus, assisting children to develop into responsible citizens will also necessitate helping them improve their own self-concepts.

Fourth, in guiding students toward creating their own rainbows, educators can help remove yet another obstacle to individual fulfillment—poor health. Today an increasing number of youth grow up in impoverished circumstances, become chemically dependent, and experiment with sex at an early age. Teachers can teach wellness and good grooming habits; they discuss the importance of nourishment and the ill effects of drugs and alcohol. The need for attention to good health has never been greater because without good health, children and adults generally will not seek fulfillment and well-being.

Attending to these four areas of concern—fear of failure, love, motivation, and health—will help children begin to create their own rainbows. Yet children also "need to understand who and what they are before they think about what they wish to become" (Gardner, 1963, p. 26). One way to help students understand their identity is to teach habits of mind that lead to usefulness in new situations. Some of these habits include curiosity, open-mindedness, objectivity, and respect for evidence (p. 27). These habits equip individuals to become more future-oriented and function effectively in a fast-paced and changing world.

In addition to helping children develop these habits of mind, parents and educators need to teach how to take responsibility for one's own happiness. Psychologist John Rosemond (1993) says this can be done by teaching children to (1) fight their own battles, (2) accept their own mistakes, (3) be persistent, (4) stand on their own feet, and (5) maximize their talents (p. 44).

More advice to parents comes from Calvin Trillin in his 1976 book *Remembering Denny*. He writes: "What my father had given me was not an even start with the sons of industrialists but something that a lot of parents manage to give their children without concocting a Grand Plan: the security that comes from knowing for sure that they believe you to be a special case" (Oder, 1993, p. 8F). We each need someone to take a special interest in us. That special someone can be a parent, relative, teacher, or friend who guides us.

Those who touch a person's life in a special way serve as a model for the rest of that person's life. Many of us can name teachers who inspired us to become who we are today. Erma Bombeck's high school teacher was a role model for her. The authors of this book can name teachers who were role models for them. Educators *can* help children and youth achieve rainbows.

We know, of course, that teachers rarely get recognition for the seeds they plant. But they can make a difference in the lives of children because teachers and education are and always will be some students' only hope.

SUMMARY

Educators can help students develop positive self-concepts, set goals, and understand how to attain their dreams or rainbows. But first educators must create their own rainbows. They do this by setting personal and professional goals, striving continuously for self-renewal, and serving as role models.

If we want to prepare children to be healthy, happy, literate, and responsible citizens, educators need to show them how to overcome obstacles to individual fulfillment. With positive self-esteem, students experience success, turn their dreams into reality, and catch a glimmer of the pot of gold at the rainbow's end.

14

Resilient Children

A certain number of the outrages upon the spirit of youth may be traced to degenerate or careless parents who totally neglect their responsibilities; a certain other large number of wrongs are due to sordid men and women who deliberately use the legitimate pleasure-seeking of young people as lures into vice. (Jane Addams, 1909, p. 51)

Many children suffer physical, social, and emotional abuse. They need vaccinations, safe homes, drug-free parents, quality schools, decent meals, and moral guidance (Geewax, 1993, December 28). America's social ills affect their well-being. They cannot avoid bringing problems into classrooms. Some survive regardless of their circumstances because they are resilient.

President Clinton reminds us these problems belong to everyone and together we must combat them. He warns that "unless we deal with the ravages of crime and drugs and violence, and unless we recognize that it's due to the breakdown of the family, the community, and the disappearance of jobs, and unless we say some of this cannot be done by government, because we have to reach deep inside the soul and the truth of human nature, none of the things we seek to do will ever take us where we need to go" (Gannon, 1993, p. 5A). Educators can help children cope with these problems by providing classroom environments conducive to enhancing their resiliency.

This chapter summarizes what research says about resiliency. It presents ideas as to how educators can help strengthen it in children and provides a historical perspective of how social problems have affected children and their resiliency.

RESILIENCY

In his book *The Art of Counseling*, Rollo May (1939) describes a young woman who grew up in an environment of family torment. After fifteen years of this one might expect her to be "a cynical, suspicious, scheming misanthrope. [But] she was an attractive, socially minded young woman, possessing more than usual amount of humor and buoyancy" (p. 35). May goes on to say: "We could cite many similar cases where the individual has used an unfavorable environment as a ladder to climb to an unusually effective personality adjustment. Bad environment increases the possibility of neurosis, but the individual may use this very potentiality for a more creative adjustment to living" (p. 35). Individuals who grow up in adverse conditions, do survive.

A report by the Northwest Regional Educational Laboratory indicates that it takes only one individual or one group to compensate for the negative influences of others ("Resilient children and," 1992). "Individuals who have succeeded in spite of adverse environmental conditions in their families, schools, and/or communities have often done so because of the presence of environmental support in the form of one family member, one teacher, one school, one community person that encouraged their success and welcomed their participation" ("Resilient children and," 1992, p. 7).

Those who succeed despite adverse conditions in the family, school, or community often share four attributes: social competence, strong problem-solving skills, autonomy, and a sense of purpose and hopefulness about the future (Benard, 1993; "Resilient children and," 1992). They are also caring, independent, and flexible; they have a sense of humor and are good at expressing their feelings; they are good learners, they have a special talent or hobby and make school a home away from home; and finally, they have a strong relationship with at least one caring adult (Harper, 1989; Smetanka, 1993). In fact, many who succeed in poor environments are "adept at finding emotional support outside the family" (Harper, 1989, p. 31).

A prime example of a resilient child who has learned the art of survival is nine-year-old streetwise Karen McCune. She is a forty-seven–pound miracle of resilience. Living in Chicago's Cabrini-Green housing, Karen avoids being in the line of sniper fire by staying indoors away from windows; she reads indoors instead of playing outside. She doesn't wear starter jackets for fear of being robbed or killed by gangbangers, and yet she has a sense of purpose—she wants to be a teacher (Will, 1992).

WHAT EDUCATORS CAN DO TO HELP STRENGTHEN CHILDREN'S RESILIENCY

Educators can help children overcome some of their problems by (1) teaching relevant subject matter using resources that reflect the reality of children's lives, (2) providing environments that foster less stress and encourage cooperative learning, (3) recognizing artistic, musical, and physical intelligence, (4) providing counseling groups, and (5) building students' self-esteem (see Chapter 13 for more information on self-esteem). The key to helping resilient children is capitalizing upon their strengths (Smetanka, 1993).

Teachers become familiar with what is and what is not normal behavior in their students. Oftentimes behavioral changes in children are connected to family problems. What can teachers do when encountering such changes in children's behavior? They can counter these changes by enhancing the characteristics of resiliency in children by

- building a trusting relationship with the child's parent(s)
- creating a sense of classroom community
- providing opportunities for the child to discuss problems in group settings
- setting limits for the child
- informing the principal and appropriate counselors of their plans for intervention
- giving the child a sense of belonging by assigning a special responsibility in the classroom (Brodkin & Coleman, 1994)

Based on a thirty-three-year study of resilient children, Werner says in *Against the Odds* (1986): "In many situations it might make better sense and be less costly as well to strengthen the available informal ties to kin and community than it would to introduce additional layers of bureaucracy into delivery of services" (in Harper, 1989, p. 31).

Perhaps the most reassuring message about helping resilient individuals is knowing that "competence, confidence and caring can flourish even under adverse circumstances if young children encounter people in their lives who provide them with a secure basis for the development of trust, autonomy and initiative" (Harper, 1989, p. 31).

Experts on helping children in crisis suggest mandatory parenting classes, adding moral and character education to early childhood programs, and getting researchers involved in real-life social issues that improve the family (Hopfensperger, 1993, October 29).

Helping children strengthen their resiliency is vital because many are fearful of the future. When the staff of the *Minneapolis Star Tribune* asked children and youth what they believed would be their greatest challenges as adults, "the vast majority of the nearly 6,200 who responded named these as the most critical challenges: the environment, crime and violence, and economic survival" (Snow, 1993, p. 1E). Regarding crime and violence, many are worried about murder, rape, gangs, and drug dealing. Snow (1993) summarizes that many of the children wrote "of being afraid they'll be assaulted or kidnapped when they're outdoors or at home alone. Many girls, especially little girls, wrote of their fears of being raped. Some suggested that in the future everyone will have to wear bulletproof vests when they go outside" (p. 3E). According to Snow, the children blame violence on the "entertainment media, drugs and the overall lack of values" (p. 3E).

In a similar survey students wrote essays about their communities, and the greatest fear they reported was crime. "It hangs over the more than 7,000 student essays like an angry, darkening cloud. For the city kids in the high-crime areas, though, the thunder about crime is the loudest and most frightening" (Monaghan, 1994, p. 1E).

Despite these fears, many children will survive because caring educators provide environments conducive to strengthening their resiliency.

A HISTORICAL PERSPECTIVE OF HOW SOCIAL PROBLEMS HAVE AFFECTED CHILDREN AND THEIR RESILIENCY

It seems children have always been resilient. Many have endured adverse conditions and hardships, yet in spite of this they have grown up to be well-adjusted adults.

Exploitation

Four centuries ago orphans, abandoned children, and youthful offenders were considered burdens by London society and became a source for settling the New World. The importation of children early in our country's history was considered "not only as a boon to the Virginia planters but as a service to king and country and a kindness to the children" (Bremner, 1970, p. 6). Documents record children as young as seven being transported to New England. Many who survived the voyage were sent to Virginia, where they worked under masters who had authority to imprison, punish, or "dispose" of the disorderly. Indentured children worked as servants or apprentices until they reached the age of twenty-one, at which time they were promised better living conditions for their years of service.

Children from countries such as the Netherlands, Germany, and Africa were also sent to the New World. The West India Company urged the importation of poor and orphaned children from the Netherlands in 1645. Colonists who brought or begot children in the New Netherlands in 1650 were allowed tax exemptions.

During colonial history "children were an integral part of the . . . labor system because the work of children was inseparable from family relationships" (Bremner, 1970, p. 103). Parents were held responsible for their children's governance. Children were involved in chores at an early age. Service, obedience, and loyalty were drilled or beaten into their minds and souls.

Children were an integral part of the labor force required during the Industrial Revolution as well. The Slater cotton mills in New England, for example, used the English plan of employing entire families. The desirability of raising a family and its economic assets were determined by the number of employable children. In 1816 90 percent of the manufacturing labor force in New England were women and children. Factories measured their efficiency in terms of necessary boy or girl power. Children as young as four were employed, working long hours with little or no schooling or recreation. But "unlike apprentices, factory children had no legal recourse in the case of abuse" (Bremner, 1970, p. 149).

Eventually laws required children who worked in manufacturing to attend school, state constitutions supported public education, and compulsory attendance was mandated.

In spite of this, even today thousands of children are without legal counsel. The American Bar Association reports that because youth today do not have legal counsel, "thousands of children [are] doomed to poverty, incarceration, poor health, no education and little hope" ("Report says children," 1993, p. 2A).

Separation from Parents

In colonial times some families were separated, with parent and child never seeing each other again. Although some children volunteered to serve as indentures, others were "spirited" away from England to America by "man-stealers," taken against the will or consent of their parents, friends, or masters (Bremner, 1970). Rebellious and neglected children were taken from parents and "bound" as servants. An example of this occurred in 1709 and 1710, when approximately 3,000 Germans displaced by the War of the Spanish Succession arrived in New York. Many were sick and poor, unable to care or work for themselves. Without the consent of parents, the governor of New York disposed of German children by binding them out. Binding was thus used as a means of social control and public welfare (Bremner, 1970).

Anyone who has read Alex Haley's *Roots* or seen the television miniseries knows all too well the horror stories of what happened to children separated from their parents in the African slave trade.

Today children placed in foster homes can be uprooted at a moment's notice. This happened to a fourteen-month-old foster child who was adopted by another family. He was given a new name, new parents, and a new house. The foster family was never to be seen again. The courts, of course, considered what was in the child's best interests, but "deep inside he'd retained the pain of that childhood separation. What the mind forgets, the heart remembers" (Kelley, 1993, p. 15A).

Another example of state-mandated separation of child and parent or guardian occurred when a judge did not award the custody of a child to its lesbian mother. Conservatives argued that this was a courageous action because the child's emotions must be protected. Advocates for lesbian and gay rights protested, declaring that "the ruling elevates bigotry, ignorance and hatefulness and denigrates a loving, life-giving relationship between a parent and child" ("Judge scorned, hailed," 1993, p. 14A).

Separation of child and parent is not always state-mandated. Many missing children today are "kidnapped," much like those spirited away by man-stealers in the 1600s. The mother of an abducted child missing for over two years writes: "Until we as a society decide to protect our children and respect the laws that were created on their behalf, the abuse will continue. . . . It's heartbreaking we keep blaming the children for their involvement with those who are so good at manipulating their innocence. Adults who prey on children have to be stopped. It's not just a moral issue. It's the law" (Wetterling, 1993, p. 28A).

There are other reasons for the separation of children and youth from their parents. Some teens run away because they "would rather be on the run than living with parents who are misusing drugs or alcohol. They would rather sleep in an abandoned building than in homes where they are abused" (Chandler, 1993, November 7, p. 2A). Other youth are thrown out of the house by their parents. To survive, these youth learn to fend for themselves, becoming prostitutes, stealing to eat, and so on. Other children are abandoned because their parent(s) cannot afford to feed and shelter them.

Abuse

Many children endure physical, sexual, emotional, and verbal abuse, although many more, of course, do not.

In colonial times, perhaps the worst abuse of children was inflicted by their masters. Children were hung up by their heels, hit on the head with meat hammers and broomsticks, whipped with "stripes," burned, bruised, and so on. Many children of Plymouth were "so oppressed with their heavy labors . . . [that they] . . . became decrepit in their early youth" (Bremner, 1970, p. 17).

An extreme and tragic example of abuse and oppression is what happened to a battered twelve-year-old boy in Plymouth in 1655. The dead boy's body was found black and blue; his back was covered with stripes; his knuckles, one big toe, and the sides of his feet were frozen; flesh was broken on his knees and heels; he lacked sufficient food, clothing, and lodging; his clothes were frozen to his body from his wetting the bed; lameness and soreness kept him from performing the required work; and so, because of hard work and cruelty, he died (Bremner, 1970). Eventually, people became outraged over these kinds of abuses. Laws were enacted to protect servants against mistreatment.

A century ago schooling took children out of the workforce but not out of an atmosphere of master dominance. Just as indentured children were punished by their masters, they were corporally punished by schoolmasters. Corporal punishment of children in school included using the whipping post and the rod, thumping the head, boxing ears, pulling hair, and even starving.

Compassionate physicians, writers, teachers, and other promoters of humanitarian reforms advocated different approaches to changing deviant behavior. As long ago as 1787 Benjamin Rush suggested that corporal punishment was hurtful, unnecessary, and contrary to the spirit of liberty; that the punished become violent toward their teachers, schooling, and others; and that the best teachers never make use of it. However, corporal punishment remains lawful in many states.

Children continue to suffer abuses, but today schools are a major source in uncovering child abuse. Educators are legally responsible for reporting to appropriate officials any suspected abuse of students with whom they work.

Ingrassia and McCormick (1994) ask, "Why leave children with bad parents? . . . [Because] last year, 1,300 abused kids died . . . [and] there were 1 million confirmed cases of abuse and neglect . . . [and] an estimated 462,000 children were in substitute care" (pp. 52–53). A study conducted by the Health and Human Services (HHS) National Center on Child Abuse and Neglect shows that "disabled children are physically and sexually abused at almost twice the rate of other children. They are emotionally neglected at almost three times the rate" ("HHH finds schools," 1993, p. 2). According to a child development expert, "children who grow up in violent homes beyond the age of 8 or 10 risk becoming so emotionally and psychologically damaged that they can never be repaired" (Ingrassia & McCormick, 1994, p. 56).

Some children are taken advantage of by those they trust. In the mid-1990s priestly pedophilia is recognized as a serious problem. The "clerical sex abuse of minors, reliably estimated by church canon lawyers and sociologists . . . number about 6 percent of the nation's 50,000 priests" (McCarthy, 1993, November 24, p. 13A).

Survival for the Basics

At the end of the nineteenth century, the wave of immigrants peaked. People with few assets came to America with dreams of a better life for themselves and their children. Many struggled without improvement, continuing a pauper's existence. Many were taken advantage of by the greedy. Children were abandoned, left to roam and fend for themselves on the streets of large cities. To care for the needy, the number of social welfare agencies and institutions continued to grow.

Educators at the turn of the twentieth century dealt with an influx of foreign students who spoke little or no English. Unfamiliar with American schooling customs, students were frightened. They were also concerned about their families' struggles for basic survival. Since bilingual education and school-related social services were not widely accepted, teaching and learning were frustrating for teachers and pupils. As a result, many students dropped out.

Today educators experience similar situations with an increasing number of non-English-speaking students in the schools. The social problems facing children are inundating classrooms (Finden, 1993; Hopfensperger, 1993, November 5). For example, one teacher said, "It's not easy to teach English to young people who have issues that take priority, like a place to live, paying their rent, eating" (Hopfensperger, 1993, November 5, p. 1B). Some children of immigrants, migrants, the homeless, and abusive parents continue to suffer physically, socially, and emotionally. The Children's Defense Fund "estimates that 100,000 American children go to sleep homeless every night" ("CDF cites violence," 1994, p. 1). In school, homeless children are restless, inattentive, tired, and hungry.

Well-Being of Children Today

Newspaper stories reflect some of the concerns about the well-being of children today: "2 Children, 2 Tragedies: Boy Accused of Murdering Crying Infant" (McWhirter, 1993); "Rare Form of Child Abuse Cited in Mother's Custody Loss" (Chandler, 1993, February 22); "It Was a Sad Time for Children Who Often Were Victims" (Schwarz, 1994). As documented in two major reports in the 1990s, children do not fare well. According to a report by the Center for the Study of Social Policy, the national trend for the well-being of children is anything but optimistic.

The report shows that a remarkable number of U.S. families—almost half—are at risk of failing right from the start for at least one of three reasons: the mother is under 20 when she has her first baby; the mother hasn't finished high school when she has her first child; or the parents of this first baby are not married. Of nearly 1.7 million new families begun in 1990, 45 percent were at risk for one or more of these reasons. Each of these risks increases the chances that families will break up, be poor, or be dependent on public assistance and that their children will be neglected and fall behind in school. (Berg, 1993, p. 1B)

We might remember, however, that for all the negatives we hear about the single-parent American family, "[single parents] are, millions of them, the unacknowledged heroes of our time. Few are single parents entirely by choice; nearly all do their best by their kids" (Tice, 1993, p. 8A).

Another report documenting the well-being of youth today is the U.S. Department of Education's study "Youth Indicators 1993: Trends in the Well-Being of American Youth." This report finds that "U.S. teenagers are holding their own in school . . . [but] . . . outside the classroom . . . they must deal with the reality of violence, AIDS, drugs, the sheer drag of poverty" ("Study finds students," 1993, p. 7A).

The well-being of children is greatly affected by violence. Children in the 1990s are most affected by gun violence: "Between 1979 and 1991, nearly 50,000 children were killed by guns, a figure roughly equivalent to the number of Americans killed in the Vietnam War" (Imig, 1994, p. 2).

As a part of a national campaign to increase our awareness of the "damage children suffer when they witness violence in their lives or are victims of it . . . the White House . . . will show anti-violence public service announcements featuring President Clinton before . . . films" (Pelton, 1994, p. 5).

CONCLUSION

The social problems of today, such as poverty, crime, illegitimacy, have always been a part of American social history. Echoes of complaints voiced by Puritans in the 1600s about the breakdown of the family continue to be heard today. In 1993 experts describe "family breakdown and the rise of illegitimacy . . . as the recognized root of America's social problems" (Gannon, 1993, p. 5A). William Doherty, a professor of family social sciences at the University of Minnesota, says: "Two things are brand new in family history . . . first that we're trying to build family around the equality of the sexes and second, that we have no broad consensus in our society about what a family should look like. And societies have always had a consensus about what a family should be" (Picone, 1993, p. 11A). Does our society agree on what the American family is? Some children live with their natural father and mother, but many do not. Examples of evolving family relationships are "my child's stepbrother; my stepmother's father; my stepsibling's father; my ex-wife's husband; my former in-law; my child's half sister; my ex-husband's wife; and, my father's ex-wife's child" (Picone, 1993, p. 11A). Little wonder children are confused.

SUMMARY

Today we are bombarded with editorials, articles, talk show programs, and documentaries concerned with the effects of contemporary family structure upon society. We hear, read, and observe that many of America's children are in trouble because of cycles of poverty, violence, and the failure of governmental institutions ("Report says children," 1993).

For centuries children have endured abuses, and through their resilience many have survived and have managed to lead healthy adult lives. Today is no different than at any other time in history. Children need to learn to manage their problems, to build their self-esteem, and to become hopeful. Capitalizing on children's strengths, educators can help their students cope and overcome some of their problems by providing environments that fortify their resiliency. Educators can indeed provide hope to children in crisis. This is most worthily noted by Sandra McBrayer, 1994 National Teacher of the Year: "My goal as a teacher is for all kids to feel that whether the world isn't caring for them or the dysfunctional parents aren't caring for them, there's a school and there are teachers that believe in them and love them" ("Teacher of year," 1994, p. 7A).

15

Teaching Nonviolence

It isn't enough to talk about peace. One must believe in it. And it isn't enough to believe in it. One must work at it. (Eleanor Roosevelt, "Voice of America," 1951)

Chapter 15 discusses the need for teaching nonviolence and peacemaking. It offers ideas on how educators can decrease violent behavior among youth, describes conflict resolution and peer mediation, provides examples of how schools are teaching nonviolence, and lists resources. It also includes a discussion of Colman McCarthy's proposal for creating an office of peace education within the U.S. Department of Education.

THE NEED FOR TEACHING NONVIOLENCE AND PEACEMAKING

Every day we hear and read about examples of violent and deviant behavior among youth: disrespect for authority, bigotry, lying, stealing, cheating, vandalizing, fighting, harassing, killing, and on and on. (Specific examples of deviant and violent behavior are documented in Chapter 1.) Society is barraged daily with an increase in violence from people of all ages, backgrounds, and socioeconomic levels. Children observe violence on television, in movies, on video games, on the streets, and in their homes. On school grounds children encounter it in the hallways, restrooms, locker rooms, and in classrooms. In fact, "ten percent of American public school teachers and nearly a fourth of students say they have been the victims of an act of violence at school" (Hamburger, 1993, p. 1A).

The mounting national public fear of violent crime in society is being heard. More school districts are hiring security personnel. Acting on the problems of gun violence and crime, President Clinton intends to take back the streets from thugs ("Clinton will stress," 1993, p. 27A). But any one institution alone cannot solve all the problems. We need to work together. At a White House prayer breakfast President Clinton said the country needs to "go forward with a deeper sense of shared values and togetherness toward the common good than we've had so far" ("Clinton calls on," 1993, p. 7A). Even though conflict can never be eradicated, we can teach people to manage conflict in nonviolent ways.

WHAT EDUCATORS CAN DO TO DECREASE VIOLENT BEHAVIOR AMONG YOUTH

One way educators decrease violent behavior among youth is by helping them meet their basic needs for safety and security. Teachers do this by creating a nonthreatening classroom climate and school environment. Such an atmosphere nurtures success, positive self-esteem, and cooperation. Students who learn to work cooperatively gain higher prosocial skills such as effective communication, conflict management, and peer mediation (Johnson & Johnson, 1975). Learning how to work with each other by resolving differences nonviolently is an outcome society wants for every citizen.

A second way educators decrease violence among youth and ensure safe schools is by preventing weapon concealment. The recency of using metal detectors in large urban school districts is described in "Fighting a War on Weapons," an article outlining the history of the use of metal detectors in schools. Porter (1993) reports:

- In 1985 Detroit was the first district to use metal detector sweeps.
- In 1987 the New York City Public Schools purchased metal detectors, and Chicago shortly followed.
- In 1993 Kansas City added detectors in all forty-four high schools *and* middle schools. The Dallas schools tripled the number of walk-through detectors, and Dade County schools hired a security company to conduct random metal detector searches.

School leaders interviewed by Porter acknowledge the use of metal detectors as a short-term solution until they are able to empower students with nonviolent strategies. But for now, they say, metal detectors help screen students' bookbags, backpacks, and baggy pants.

A third way educators contribute to decreasing the amount of violence among youth is by promoting responsible and respectful behavior. This can be done in various ways. One way is by setting school standards for acceptable behavior. Three such standards might include (1) honoring the sanctity of other people's property and space; (2) enforcing behavior that is gender-fair, disability-sensitive, and respectful of diversity; and (3) encouraging school language that is free from sexual slang, swearing, and other expressions intended or interpreted as offensive.

Promoting responsible and respectful behavior can also be done by infusing character education into the curriculum. The Character Education Institute in San Antonio, Texas, promotes an instructional program that teaches children to be values-literate. Most of these values are universal and worthy of educators' attention. The Character Education Curriculum enables children and youth to do the following:

- Respect the rights of others.
- Distinguish between "right" and "wrong."
- Work together cooperatively.
- Identify the rights and obligations of citizens.
- Develop decision-making and problem-solving skills.
- Assume responsibility for their behavior.
- Maximize the use of their time and talents. (Mulkey, 1992, p. 4)

Many of these values have been discussed throughout this book as strategies for reducing intolerance but most of all for creating hope.

Yet another way to promote respectful and responsible behavior is by teaching conflict resolution and peer mediation. These strategies help students learn to resolve differences in nonviolent ways and become responsible for their own behavior. (Conflict resolution and peer mediation are described later in this chapter.)

Getting back to how educators can decrease violence among youth, a preventive strategy they might use is managing crisis interventions. They do this by defusing potential crises through recognition of "situations that can lead to disruptive, assaultive or out of control behaviors" (Gundlach, 1993, p. 10). Teachers who prevent crises look for three key behaviors likely to increase anxiety among youth: (1) invasion of personal space, (2) misinterpretation of body language, and (3) miscommunication (Gundlach, 1993).

A fifth way teachers help reduce violence among youth is by helping them learn to cope with violence. Professionals can do four things to provide for the needs of children and youth who have no choice but to cope with violence outside the classroom. They can (1) help youth develop meaningful relationships with caring adults; (2) provide organized and consistent schedules; (3) communicate explicit expectations and limits for activities and behavior; and (4) offer opportunities for expression, such as play, expressive art, and storytelling (Wallach, 1993).

Finally, teachers can decrease violence by teaching their students to use rules like the following when solving communication problems:

- State your own feelings clearly, without being accusatory. Begin with "I feel . . ." instead of "You always . . ."
- Never interrupt or finish another person's sentences.
- Concentrate on what is being said to you, rather than on your response.
- Maintain eye contact with the other person.
- Ask questions to clarify what the other person is saying.
- Repeat the other person's ideas as you understand them.
- Never put anyone down. (Meek, 1992, p. 49).

These skills—being able to listen and articulate the feelings of another person—are the core of conflict resolution.

CONFLICT RESOLUTION AND PEER MEDIATION

"Conflict is a situation or state between at least two interdependent parties, . . . is an inevitable and all-pervasive element in our society . . . [and] allows us to learn, progress, and grow" (Katz & Lawyer, 1993, p. 7). Conflict itself is not bad. But when avoided or unresolved, it is (Johnson, Johnson, Dudley, & Burnett, 1992; Katz & Lawyer, 1993). Positive or negative consequences can result from conflict, depending upon how it is managed. Some positive consequences are reconciliation of the interests of the disputing parties, a sharpened sense of identity and solidarity, interaction, internal change, and clarification of the real problem. Negative consequences of unresolved conflict might include minor differences escalating into major ones, an increase in the number of differences, specifics giving way to global concerns, and an increase in the number of parties involved (Katz & Lawyer, 1993).

Educators must, if they hope to teach these skills to children and youth, be role models in the resolution of controversies among themselves, between students, and between themselves and parents (Scherer, 1992). For example, in teacher-teacher conflicts, administrators must mediate in a positive way so that a resolution is achieved. Likewise, teacher-administrator conflicts must be resolved peacefully. In their book *Conflict Resolution: Building Bridges*, Katz and Lawyer (1993) list ten attitudes for the successful resolution of conflict.

1. Unconditional positive regard of others involved in a conflict
2. Proactivity, one of taking initiative and making things happen

3. Being soft on people and hard on the problem [attack the problem, not the people]
4. Being unconditionally constructive in a conflict situation
5. Being vision driven and outcome oriented
6. A win/win frame of reference
7. Openness, respect, and appreciation for diversity
8. Trust as the primary foundation of relationships
9. Learning from experience as a key to increasing autonomy [taking control of one's own destiny]
10. Viewing conflict as an opportunity for personal growth and development. (p. 21)

Holding a positive attitude toward conflict and its resolution is essential. In the Peacemaker Program, Johnson et al. (1992) teach peer mediators and students several rules, including the following: no name calling, no interruptions, doing what is agreed upon, being honest, and retaining confidentiality. When students fail to negotiate a conflict, the following chain of mediators is employed: peer mediator, then the teacher, and if necessary the principal.

Conflict resolution and peer mediation programs *are* making a difference (Johnson et al., 1992; Meek, 1992; Moore & Beland, 1992). Such programs empower people in many ways. Research shows that those who receive training are by and large able to resolve conflicts without the help of others, master negotiation and mediation skills and procedures, and use these skills in other settings (Johnson et al., 1992; Meek, 1992; Moore & Beland, 1992).

As a part of the training process students must first learn to regulate their own behavior. In order to do this: "[they] must monitor their own behavior, assess situations, make judgments as to which behaviors are appropriate, and master the procedures and skills required to engage in desired behavior. [Students] . . . must have opportunities to (1) make decisions regarding how to behave and (2) follow through on the decisions made" (Johnson et al., 1992, p. 10). When given such opportunities, children and youth monitor their own behavior more effectively than those who receive no training, and they gain empathy for others' perspectives.

Many peer mediation programs are designed to help friends help friends. Such programs teach the skills of helping self and others, for setting limits, and of resolving differences through negotiation. These programs benefit schools and society by improving school climate; enabling students to develop lifelong skills for helping peers and self; bringing fewer minor problems to educators, thus allowing them to focus on major concerns; and developing positive student attributes and skills in leadership, communication, problem solving, and critical thinking (Gundlach, 1993; Johnson et al., 1992; Stephens, 1993).

EXAMPLES OF SCHOOLS TEACHING NONVIOLENCE

Many of the nation's schools are now teaching nonviolent ways to resolve disputes or require a course in conflict resolution. A glance through professional education journals indicates that the number of schools offering peer mediation classes is on the rise. One example of a school offering peer mediation is Patrick Henry High School in Minneapolis, Minnesota, where seventy-five students each year take a course in conflict resolution. Students who fight are suspended, returning to school only after using the mediation process (Grow, 1993). The past five years have seen a dramatic decrease in suspensions.

After a 1990 riot at Cleveland High School in Reseda, California, a drama teacher headed an antiviolence project that enlists students who work on committees "to reduce racial tension and increase cultural sensitivity. Students who once led the conflict, now take the lead in preventing it" (Merina, 1993, p. 5). Natural leaders, including athletes, student body representatives, and gang members, representing the school's diverse student body, are selected as mediators. The empowered students learn alternatives to solving conflicts. Testimonial to their success was a school dance organized by African-American and Latino students. The event, described by Cleveland's drama teacher, "was the first time the two groups mixed together, the first time we've had a dance with no incidents, and the first time we've ever had a dance after dark" (Merina, 1993, p. 5).

Another example of a high school system teaching nonviolence is the Kansas City Public Schools. They employ a youth court where crimes are judged by peers. It is the hope of Kansas City educators that a sense of crime and punishment will carry over into the rest of the students' lives (Porter, 1993).

Some school districts are also teaching nonviolent strategies for resolving conflict to younger students. For example, fourth-, fifth-, and sixth-graders at Ketcham Elementary School in Washington, D.C., are trained in conflict management techniques by the National Institute for Citizen Education in the Law. Since its inception at Ketcham, the training program has helped students resolve verbal conflicts and physical confrontations in the classroom and on the playground ("Elementary school students," 1991). Perhaps the most important aspect of this program is the level of community involvement. Student managers are sworn in by a D.C. Superior Court Judge and receive certificates from the D.C. Center Director. Obviously, this is a "big deal" to the students who are rewarded by being good.

At Orchards Elementary School, near Lewiston, Idaho, educators reported that students were bringing problems from home to school and acting out their frustrations and anger on each other and on their teachers. Teachers began teaching problem solving and conflict resolution. As a result, students gained respect for themselves and others. Now student managers help their peers handle problems in the classroom and on the playground (Merina, 1993).

And at Highlands Elementary School in Edina, Minnesota, students receive thirty minutes of training each day for six weeks to become peace-makers through the curriculum *Teaching Students to Be Peacemakers* (Johnson & Johnson, 1991). Through a three-step process students are taught negotiation, mediation, and peacemaking skills and procedures (Johnson et al., 1992).

Even as early as preschool and kindergarten, some school districts are teaching violence prevention. Through a program called Second Step, students learn how to empathize, control their impulses, and manage their anger. Teachers help students use these skills in real situations. This program is an extension of the Committee for Children's Violence Prevention programs for older children (Moore & Beland, 1992).

An example of how the Second Step Program works is described in a *Chicago Sun-Times* editorial about Anne Parry, who teaches three- and four-year-olds in the Head Start Program, their teachers, and their parents how to express anger without violence ("Nonviolence course is," 1993). According to this editorial, the program is: "one of many positive efforts to counter the growing incidence of children being murdered and committing crimes. Kids who are bombarded with violence on TV, in their neighborhoods and sometimes from their families need to learn nonviolent ways to vent their frustrations. And they need to learn [them] early" (p. 21). School leaders in other cities such as Durham, North Carolina, where each day students encounter neighborhood violence, are also reaching out to educate community agencies and parents about conflict resolution (Merina, 1993).

These are only a few examples of schools and programs teaching nonviolence. It is not too late to implement conflict resolution and peer mediation programs in any school or district. As one hopeful teacher said, "We have to start somewhere."

CASE FOR AN OFFICE OF PEACE EDUCATION

The case for teaching nonviolence has been made throughout much of this book. A decline in moral standards, increased levels of intolerance and greed, and an escalation of violence in our country are symptomatic of a society that is peace illiterate. As an advocate for peace, Colman McCarthy (1992), syndicated *Washington Post* columnist and director of the Center for Teaching Peace, succinctly describes the results of peace illiteracy. He states, "We are peace illiterates all but helpless to deal with conflicts in families, schools, neighborhoods or among governments in any way except the failed methods of fists, guns, armies and threats" (p. 14A).

McCarthy's solution is an office of peace education within the U.S. Department of Education. He envisions it as a resource center for educators, students, and parents to begin or expand curriculum in conflict resolution and peacemaking at all grade levels. The need for such an office is well documented by the increase in violence. Daily children and youth face conflict at home, in the classroom, on the playground, and in the neighborhood. As adults they also experience controversy in social and political relationships at home, in the workplace, and with the government. Yet they are not taught how to manage conflict in positive ways (McCarthy, 1993, August 5).

The authors of this book believe McCarthy's proposal has merit. Not only do children, youth, and parents need to be taught how to resolve conflicts peacefully, but so do some educators! This area of education has been neglected.

In years past, when there was no mandatory curriculum in conflict resolution and when teaching "morals" was a part of home and school curricula, students learned to respect themselves and others and learned how to get along with people. But today many students are not taught values in the home. Educators have to work with students who bring a host of problems with them into the classroom. Educators need to know how to teach skills to solve problems in a nonviolent manner. Research shows that once students learn to solve their own problems peaceably, teachers spend less time on discipline and more time on instruction. Since students learn through observation and modeling, teachers, administrators, and counselors need to be role models for settling disputes peacefully. Therefore, an office of peace education with resources to prepare not only students and parents but especially educators is a viable means to accomplish this imperative task.

SUMMARY

Violence and crime take a toll on our society. Educators need to model and teach peaceful ways of resolving conflicts. Conflict resolution and peer mediation programs have been adopted by some schools. The results of these programs are positive.

There are many resources, including books, articles, curriculum implementation guides, manuals, videos, institutes, and workshops, available for preschool to adult conflict resolution training.

A few organizations and publishers who have resources available are listed below.

ABA Special Committee on Dispute Resolution, School Mediation Clearinghouse
1800 M Street N.W.
Washington, DC 20036

Association for Supervision and Curriculum Development
1250 N. Pitt Street
Alexandria, VA 22314

Center for Teaching Peace
4501 Van Ness St., N.W.
Washington, DC 20016

Character Education Institute
8918 Tesoro Drive, Suite 220
San Antonio, TX 78217–6253

**Children's Creative Response to
Conflict Program**
Fellowship of Reconciliation
Box 271
Nyack, NY 10960

Committee for Children
172 20th Avenue
Seattle, WA 98122

The Community Board Program
1540 Market Street, Suite 490
San Francisco, CA 94102

Corwin Press, Inc.
2455 Teller Road
Newbury Park, CA 91320

Educators for Social Responsibility
School Conflict Resolution Programs
23 Garden St.
Cambridge, MA 02138

**National Association for Mediation in Education
(NAME)**
425 Amity Street
Amherst, MA 01002

**National Conference on Peacemaking and Conflict
Resolution**
George Mason University
4400 University Drive
Fairfax, VA 22030

National Institute for Citizen Education in the Law
One Dupont Circle, N.W., Suite 200
Washington, DC 20036–1166

**Project SMART (School Mediators' Alternative
Resolution Team)**
2 Lafayette Street
New York, NY 10007

Resolving Conflict Creatively
New York City Public Schools
163 Third Avenue, #239
New York, NY 10003

Teaching Students to Be Peacemakers
Cooperative Learning Center
150 Pillsbury Dr., S.E.
Minneapolis, MN 55455–2098

16

America's Least Expensive, Most Powerful, Most Available Resource: Reading Aloud

When kids are sheltered from the consequences of failure and inappropriate behavior, it shouldn't surprise anyone when they grow up and flunk out of school, get fired from jobs or wind up in trouble with the law. When they learn to abide by rational rules and standards, on the other hand, they have a head start in life. ("Discipline gives kids," 1993, p. 12)

Today some young people kill casually, giving it no more thought than unwrapping and chewing a stick of gum. For them human life has no value, and after killing they feel no remorse. They respect neither the police nor any other adult with authority. "Nationally, the number of *murder* arrests for those 17 years and younger increased 85 percent from 1987 to 1991" (Griffin, 1993, p. 11A).

Not all young people, of course, act out the anger they feel, nor do all lack the ability to empathize. In fact, many are victims themselves. But large numbers of children today—especially those raised by the television set and by other children—desperately need, for their own sake and for society's sake, exposure to socially acceptable models and examples of civilized behavior. Young people need to be introduced to values extolling patience, self-discipline, fair play, and tolerance.

Although we will never be able to guarantee a safe America for everyone, we can begin to save ourselves by turning off the spigot that keeps spewing out new violence-prone youngsters (Raspberry, 1993, August 20,

p. 17A). A step, perhaps a mere step, but nonetheless a step in the right direction, is to do something as ordinary and simple as reading aloud to children.

Reading aloud awakens the imagination and allows it to soar. It permits children to dream and to be hopeful. It connects children with something universal and provides an opportunity to share experiences common among all humans (Maxwell, 1993). Allowing students to see the viewpoints of other groups provides a foundation for resolving conflict without violence. It also develops "habits of thought that generate alternatives to violent behavior" (Yates, 1994, p. 8). It is the least expensive, most powerful, and most available educational resource we have (" 'Read Aloud' campaign," 1991).

Reading aloud should not be allowed to become a lost art. Problems surround youth today, and now more than ever students need exposure to great minds, articulate writers, and cultured behaviors.

Children's most persistent beliefs about themselves and others are formed by the stories they hear, especially stories heard while in a group. Many years ago Spinoza said: "An emotion can neither be hindered nor moved save by a contrary emotion. Group action provides the contrary emotion" (Tenenbaum, 1947, pp. 343–344).

Tenenbaum (1947) further explains Spinoza's view as follows: "Opinions and attitudes are developed in small groups, from face-to-face contact. A person who has prejudices very often needs those prejudices to give meaning and security to his life; they are necessary for his well-being. Such persons are loath to surrender prejudices. In 'action-research' [such a person] is more apt to find a new orientation, to transfer his old emotionalized outlooks to new emotionalized outlooks" (p. 344).

When in a group, individuals are forced to respond to the reactions of others. If, for example, an individual laughs when everyone cries, the person laughing immediately senses that he or she may have misheard; but if an individual laughs when every else laughs, or cries when everyone else cries, that individual feels in sync with the group. His or her reactions are validated and reinforced, and the attitudes learned during this exchange are internalized.

The process is very subtle, much like that which occurs during a faculty meeting. If we are criticized and those at the meeting seem to agree with the criticism and verbally and nonverbally express agreement with the person criticizing us, we instantly and automatically question ourselves. Even the most devout existentialists among us are forced to reexamine what they have just said. But if our colleagues disagree with the criticism and shake their heads in disagreement, we assume we are correct, so that the attitudes that fostered our position become further entrenched.

If teachers choose material with care, taking into account the age, maturity, and interests of their students, and if they present this material in an interesting manner, reading aloud can affect students in positive ways never envisioned. It can help them "appreciate certain virtues, such as self-sacrifice, loyalty, and the democratic ideals of freedom and equality" (Rosemond, 1992, p. 34). It can assist them in beginning the critical thinking process by helping them to be "disposed to question, to examine, to suspend judgment until the available evidence is weighed" (Walsh, 1991, p. 26). It can significantly broaden their reading interests and tastes (Kimmel & Segel, 1983). It can also condition students to believe that reading is a pleasurable experience (Trelease, 1989).

Like many of you, we can remember hearing stories read aloud in school. As a fifth-grader, one of the authors remembers hearing a much longer version of the following story being read aloud in class:

The setting was a Canadian cabin during winter.

A man's wife had just died and he was left alone to raise their infant daughter. Food ran out, so he wrapped his child in blankets, placed wood on the fire, and told the family's German shepherd, "Guard Sarah with your life." He then left for supplies.

A violent storm delayed his return for many, many days. Finally he returned, opened the cabin door, and there on the floor was his daughter's overturned crib, and no sign of his baby girl. His dog lay curled on the floor covered with blood. His own starving animal had eaten her!

Enraged, he dragged the whimpering German shepherd from the cabin and shot him until his revolver was empty. He then sobbed violently until darkness. Finally, he crawled into the cabin.

Suddenly he heard something, a faint cry. Rushing to the overturned crib, he threw it aside and there on the floor lay his infant daughter, alive, still wrapped in her bedclothes. Behind her and beside her were the bloody and mangled bodies of three dead half-starved wolves.

Indeed his German shepherd had guarded Sarah with his life.

Each day one of the teachers in our rural schools read aloud to us for twenty minutes. During this period, we listened to short stories, poems, and many English and American classics. Robert Louis Stevenson's *Treasure Island*, Harriet Beecher Stowe's *Uncle Tom's Cabin*, Longfellow's *Evangeline*, Mark Twain's *Adventures of Tom Sawyer*, Willa Cather's *O Pioneers*, and James Fenimore Cooper's *Deerslayer* are a few that come easily to mind. During this formative period we were ready for profound ideas and deeper thinking. This, of course, is true of youngsters today as well.

We and our fellow classmates were allowed to create our own images and be the heroes of every story. Our imagination was given wings. We were allowed to reflect and dream. An appeal was made to the best that was in us. We were exposed to values that would become a part of us and remain long after the details of daily lessons were forgotten.

In this pliable stage we were exposed to noble ideas, to magnificent speeches, and to authors whose skill enabled them to say exactly what they wished to say and to affect listeners precisely as they intended. Such artists uplifted our expectations and hopes. We ourselves assumed the humility, mercy, courage, and boldness of the characters; we wished to emulate those who spoke out to say what needed saying, and we admired those who did the "right thing" even if it meant being unpopular. The concreteness of an image was not allowed to interfere with our fantasies.

Through literature our teachers tried to prepare us for good and evil and for unfairness. They helped us to become more accepting of ideas different from our own. They encouraged us to exercise leadership for the common good. They exposed us to slices of life much bigger than the one in which we were living. They helped us put our lives into perspective. They appealed to our need to give and make a positive contribution to the world. They presented us with a sense of what would come in life—joy, sorrow, love, jealously, happiness, failure, disappointment, sacrifice. They showed us that we could not escape the consequences of our decisions.

Do middle school and high school teachers still read to their students, or has reading aloud become a lost art? As university supervisors of student teachers, we visit middle schools, junior high schools, and senior high schools each day and rarely see teachers reading to their students. Has the need to cover all the material by the end of the term driven out reading aloud? Is reading aloud absent because measuring and weighing that which is learned aurally is difficult? Has our exposure to boring materials read by boring speakers brought the demise of this practice? Or has knowing that children are already overstimulated and overentertained by television convinced us that oral reading no longer has a place in schools?

It is unfortunate that reading aloud to students plays such a minor role in our schools today because stories carefully selected and skillfully presented by teachers, who enjoy what they are reading and know what appeals to their students, can influence values and attitudes beyond imagination. "Reading aloud should continue all through the school years" (Kimmel & Segel, 1983, p. 12).

In closing, allow us to "read" from a local newspaper. Imagine you are a graduate student and your professor is attempting to provide a partial foundation for discussing empathy.

Elderly Poor Face Inflation and Loneliness

Emma's doctor told her she was wrong to leave the hospital so quickly after a bout with heart trouble, but Emma, 83, did not listen. After four days in the hospital, she knew she could not afford another day. . . .

She has been frugal for the many years since her husband died while she was still raising their three children. She can't remember, now, how long that has been.

"I had my last son in that room, there," she said pointing beyond the ironing board leaning against the living room closet door.

Apparently Emma now keeps most of the things she needs easily accessible in her small living room. She spends most of her time there.

"The arthritis in my knees is so bad, I can't go across the room without crutches," adding that she tries to take as few pain pills as possible because they are expensive. . . .

In spite of the pain, however, Emma still washes her clothes on a scrub board in the kitchen sink and shakes out the throw rug that sits on the linoleum living room floor "when I can," Emma said.

Once a day a neighbor brings a pail of water which is poured into the sink—"half for washing dishes and half for washing hands," Emma explained.

The neighbor also empties the pail that is a toilet, and Tommy's pan, which Emma brags her cat always uses.

"He's a good cat, that Tommy is," she said. "He's not dirty. He goes in his pan in the bathroom. And he's not snoopy. Him's my baby."

Food is a real problem for Emma, too. She says she cannot afford much of it, especially in the winter when she must buy fuel oil. "I know I need one good meal a day," she said, so she orders a "meal-on-wheels," which is delivered to her home by county workers every noon.

Often Emma eats part of the $1.50 meal and saves the rest for supper. If she eats the entire meal at noon, she may have a bread sandwich for supper.

"I get awful lonesome," she said, pulling Tommy onto her lap. Although she has an old black and white television set and a radio, neither work and she cannot afford to have them repaired. She can't read because her eyes are failing, and she can't sew because she can't afford material. (Marksjarves, 1978)

Students never outgrow their need to be read to, and reading aloud should not become a lost art. "One of the greatest gifts adults can give—to their offspring and to their society—is to read to children" (Sagan & Druyan, 1994, p. 5). Indeed, reading aloud can be one of America's greatest educational self-help programs (" 'Read-Aloud' campaign," 1991).

SUGGESTED READING

Many books are available that suggest materials to read aloud to students. You may wish to examine the following five: William F. Russell's *Classics to Read Aloud to Your Children* and *More Classics to Read Aloud to Your Children;* Margaret May Kimmel and Elizabeth Segel's *For Reading out Loud!;* Jim Trelease's *New Read-Aloud Handbook; and William Bennett's Book of Virtues.*

References

Abrams, G. (1993, January 1). Movement grows to teach the difference between right, wrong. *Minneapolis Star Tribune*, p. 10Ex.

Actress slashed by gang on N.Y. street. (1990, January 14). *Minneapolis Star Tribune*, p. 26A.

Addams, J. (1909). *The spirit of youth and the city streets*. New York: Macmillan.

Agency can't investigate air bags. (1992, June 15). *The Free Press* (Mankato, MN), p. 3.

Albert, E., Denise, T., & Peterfreund, S. (1953). *Great traditions in ethics*. New York: American Book Company.

Allain, V. (1992, October 22). *Futurism*. A presentation given to the Mankato State University Chapter of Phi Delta Kappa.

Americans help restore hope. (1992, December 13). *Omaha World-Herald*, p. 32.

Anderson, D., Major, R., & Mitchell, R. (1992). *Teacher supervision that works: A guide for university supervisors*. New York: Praeger.

The army focuses on ethics. HQDA (SAPA-CI/CIP). Office of the Chief of Public Affairs, 1500 Army Pentagon 2D622, Washington, DC.

As violence in Denver spreads, traditional reasons ring hollow. (1993, August 18). *Omaha World-Herald*, p. 18.

Ashmore, R., & Starr, W. (Eds.). (1991). *Ethics across the curriculum: The Marquette Experience*. Milwaukee, WI: Marquette University Press.

Banner, W. (1968). *Ethics: An introduction to moral philosophy*. New York: Charles Scribner & Sons.

Baptists say ouster erodes freedoms. (1992, June 12). *The Free Press* (Mankato, MN), p. 7.

Barlett, D., & Steele, J. (1992). *America: What went wrong?* Kansas City, MO: Andrews & McKeel.

Beach mob torches emergency vehicles. (1986, September 2). *The Free Press* (Mankato, MN), p. 30.

Belok, M., Bontrager, O., Oswald, H., Morris, M., & Erickson, E. (1966). *Approaches to values in education.* Dubuque, IA: William C. Brown.

Benard, B. (1993). Fostering resiliency in kids. *Educational Leadership, 51*(3), 44–45.

Bennett, W. (1993). *The book of virtues.* New York: Simon & Schuster.

Benson, G. (1982). *Business ethics in America.* Lexington, MA: Lexington Books, D. C. Heath.

Berg, S. (1993, March 29). How kids fare: Minnesota children are relatively well off, but study says happy future far from certain. *Minneapolis Star Tribune,* pp. 1B, 6B.

Berry, W. (1981). *The gift of good land.* San Francisco, CA: North Point Press.

Big-city crime goes country: Drugs, gangs taking a toll in rural areas. (1993, March 25). *Omaha World-Herald,* p. 12.

Bobbitt, F. (1918). *The curriculum.* Boston: Houghton.

Bombeck, E. (1992, November 8). Newest sickos: Purse thieves in restrooms. *Sunday Omaha World-Herald,* p. 3E.

Bombeck, E. (1992, December 3). Great teacher creates dream, changes life. *The Free Press* (Mankato, MN), p. 8.

Bonner, B. (1994, February 20). Land of hope, lure of crime. *Saint Paul Pioneer Press,* p. 14A.

Botstein, L. (1993). The use and misuse of hope. *Education Week, 12*(39), pp. 40, 48.

Bovee, T. (1993, January 28). Census study shows college diploma worth extra $1,039 a month in pay, on average. *Saint Paul Pioneer Press,* p. 2A.

Bowie, N., & Duska, R. (1990). *Business ethics.* Englewood Cliffs, NJ: Prentice Hall.

Boyd, M. (1992, June-July). On taking control. *ModernMaturity,* p. 72.

Boys accused of assaulting 5–year-old girl. (1992, March 14). *The Free Press* (Mankato, MN), p. 14.

Boys use gun to rob girl, 9. (1988, March 2). *The Free Press* (Mankato, MN), p. 3.

Brain trust: Study confirms education pays off in lifetime income. (1992, August 19). *Minneapolis Star Tribune,* p. 1A.

Bremner, R. H. (1970). *Children and youth in America: A documentary history. Volume I: 1600–1865.* Cambridge, MA: Harvard University Press.

Brodkin, A., & Coleman, M. (1994). Helping children cope with loss. *Instructor. 103*(5), pp. 24–25.

Brown, M. (1991). *Working ethics.* San Francisco: Jossey-Bass.

Brown vs. Board of Education of Topeka, Kansas. (1955, May 31). 75 SCt 753, 349 U.S. 294.

Bull, B. (1990). The limits of teacher professionalization. In J. Goodlad, R. Soder & K. Sirotnik (Eds.), *The moral dimensions of teaching* (pp. 87–129). San Francisco: Jossey-Bass.

Byron, K. H. (1965). *The pessimism of James Thomson (B.V.): In relation to his times.* Hague, Netherlands: Mouton.

Cabell, J. (1986). In H. Rawson & M. Miner (Eds.), *The New International Dictionary of Quotations* (p. 209). New York: E. P. Hutton.

Car jacking survivor recalls terror. (1992, December 3). *The Free Press* (Mankato, MN), p. 3.

Car windows shot out in spree. (1993, March 10). *The Free Press* (Mankato, MN), p. 13.

Carroll, J. (1992, June 30). Rudeness is rising rapidly; some blame it on the economy. *Minneapolis Star Tribune*, p. 3E.

Carson, R. (1962). *Silent Spring*. Boston: Houghton Mifflin.

CDF cites violence, calls for "cease fire" against children. (1994). *Education USA*, 36(11), 1.

Chandler, K. (1993, February 22). Rare form of child abuse cited in mother's custody loss. *Minneapolis Star Tribune*, pp. 1B, 5B.

Chandler, K. (1993, November 7). Homeless kids find help from a man named River. *Minneapolis Star Tribune*, pp. 1A, 2A, 23A.

Charmaine in charge. (1992, December 2). *The Free Press* (Mankato, MN), p. 1.

Church, G. J. (1992, May 11). Cover stories. *Time*, p. 20.

Civil Rights Act of 1964. (Griffin vs. County School Board of Prince Edward County et al.). (1964, May 25). 84 SCt 1226, 377 U.S. 218.

Clinton: A "crisis of spirit" grips us. (1993, November 14). *Minneapolis Star Tribune*, pp. 1A, 16A.

Clinton calls on Americans to work together. (1993, August 31). *Minneapolis Star Tribune*, p. 7A.

Clinton inaugural. (1993, January 21). *Minneapolis Star Tribune*, p. 16A.

Clinton will stress crime, gun violence. (1993, November 28). *Minneapolis Star Tribune*, p. 27A.

Close, F. (1993, Fall). Teaching values is defending our moral heritage. *Ethics Journal*, p. 3.

The code of ethics for Minnesota teachers. (1994). *MinnesotaBoard of Teaching Rules*. Executive Secretary, Minnesota Board of Teaching, 608 Capitol Square Building, 550 Cedar Street, St. Paul, Minnesota.

Colson, L. (1992, November 22). A teacher quietly plants a seed, sees it blossom. *Minneapolis Star Tribune*, p. 37A.

Command information packet. (1993). Army Office of the Chief of Public Affairs, HQDA (SAPA A-ACL/CIP), Pentagon 2D622, Washington, DC.

Constitutional Rights Foundation. (1992, Winter). Does the criminal justice system discriminate against African-Americans? *Bill of Rights in Action*, 9(1), 6.

Covey, S. (1990). *The seven habits of highly effective people*. New York: Simon & Schuster.

Cyclone warning system. (1994, May 3). *The Free Press* (Mankato, MN), p. 3.

Dear Abby. (1992, June 10). *The Free Press* (Mankato, MN), p. 26.

DeGeorge, R. (1969). *Soviet ethics and morality*. Ann Arbor, MI: University of Michigan Press.

Dewey, J. (1916). *Democracy and education*. New York: Macmillan.

Diana pleads for acts of kindness. (1993, November 19). *The Free Press* (Mankato, MN), p. 2.

Diaz, K. (1992, November 8). Domino's delivery man killed in area he'd tried to help. *Minneapolis Star Tribune*, p. 1A.

Diaz, K. (1993, March 8). Broomball jersey highlights race issues in Eden Prairie. *Minneapolis Star Tribune*, p. 1B.

Dimma, W. (1991, February 1). The decline of ethics. *Vital Speeches of the Day*, 57(8), 245.

Discipline gives kids good start. (1993, August 14). *Omaha World-Herald*, p. 12.

Doherty, W. (1993, December 6). In L. Picone. The evolving family. *Minneapolis Star Tribune*, p. 11A.

Donagan, A. (1977). *The theory of morality*. Chicago: University of Chicago Press.

Donations help flood-ravaged town. (1993, December 24). *Las Vegas Review-Journal/Sun*, p. 10A.

Donations to repair memorial pour in. (1988, May 28). *The Free Press* (Mankato, MN), p. 1.

Dowd, M. (1993, May 22). Fear of sexual violence root of outcry by women. *The Free Press* (Mankato, MN), p. 5.

Dreikurs, R. (1968). *Psychology in the classroom*. New York: Harper & Row.

Eck, D. (1992, July 4). America: Melting pot of religions. *Omaha World-Herald*, p. 14.

Education for All Handicapped Children Act of 1975. U.S. Statutes at Large, 89 Stat. 773.

8 children killed in Rio; cop suspected. (1993, July 24). *The Free Press* (Mankato, MN), p. 3.

Elam, S., Rose, L., & Gallup, A. (1993, October). Of the public's attitudes toward public schools: 25th annual PDK Gallop Poll. *Phi Delta Kappan*, 75(2), 137–152.

Elementary school students settle peer disputes. (1991). *Street Law News*. Newsletter of the National Institute for Citizen Education in the Law. Washington, DC.

Eyre, L., & Eyre, R. (1993). *Teaching your children values*. New York: Simon & Schuster.

Faulkner, W. (1959). In F. Gwynn & J. Blotner (Eds.), *Faulkner in the university* (p. 78). Charlottesville, VA: University of Virginia Press.

FBI may try to quell carjackings. (1992, September 14). *The Free Press* (Mankato, MN), p. 3.

Feinberg, W. (1990). The moral responsibility of public schools. In J. Goodlad, R. Soder, & K. Sirotnik (Eds.), *The moral dimensions of teaching* (pp. 158–187). San Francisco: Jossey-Bass.

$50,000 lost in sweepstakes scam. (1993, August 30). *The Free Press* (Mankato, MN), p. 3.

Finden, D. (1993). Hold the hot air, pass the sandbags. *Excellence* (Minnesota Federation of Teachers), 2(1), 18.

Finken, Z. (1993, August 20). Bluffs robbers prey on elderly motorists. *Omaha World-Herald*, p. 12.

Firm wants to put giant billboard in space. (1993, April 15). *Omaha World-Herald*, p. 12.

Flanery, J. (1993, August 18). State health chief urges war on epidemic of youth violence. *Omaha World-Herald*, p. 1.

Food stamp participation rising. (1992, October 31). *The Free Press* (Mankato, MN), p. 3.

Friend: McDonald's killer "was crying for help." (1993, August 12). *The Free Press* (Mankato, MN), p. 3.

Fromm, E. (1965). *Escape from freedom*. New York: Avon Books.

Fruhling, L. (1992, July 4). Gay-bashing pastor, followers keep city in Kansas in an uproar. *The Des Moines Register*, p. 3A.

Gannon, J. (1993, December 30). Idea of the year: Family breakdown. *The Des Moines Register*, p. 5A.

Gardner, J. (1963). *Self-Renewal: The individual and the innovative society.* New York: Perennial Library, Harper & Row.

Garmston, R., Linder, C., & Whitaker, J. (1993). Reflections on cognitive coaching. *Educational Leadership, 51*(2), 57–61.

Geewax, M. (1993, August 24). They might be packing guns: "Nation afraid to discipline unruly children." *Omaha World-Herald*, p. 9.

Geewax, M. (1993, December 28). The children need more than toys. *Omaha World-Herald*, p. 6.

Giroux, A., Penna, A., & Pinar, W. (Eds.). (1981). *Curriculum & instruction: Alternatives in education.* Berkeley, CA: McCutchan.

Goldstein, S. (1993, April 19). Riches spent on self-indulgence could fund neglected essentials. *Saint Paul Pioneer Press*, p. 7A.

Goodgame, D. (1990, July 16). Getting farmers off the dole. *Time*, p. 26.

Goodlad, J., Soder, R., & Sirotnik, K. (Eds.). (1990). *The moral dimensions of teaching.* San Francisco: Jossey-Bass.

Goodman, E. (1988, June 7). Intact single-parent families. *The Free Press* (Mankato, MN), p. 5.

Goodman, E. (1993, April 6). Mia vs. Woody: Psychology's inability to define morality. *The Free Press* (Mankato, MN), p. 4.

Goodwin, A. (1992, November 4). Alternative school helps paint scenario of hope for troubled teen mothers. *St. Paul Pioneer Press*, p. 16A.

Greene B. (1991, January 12). Tale of hospital theft has a familiar ring. *The Free Press* (Mankato, MN), p. 5.

Greene, B. (1992, September 8). A sad sign of the times. *The Free Press* (Mankato, MN), p. 5.

Greene, B. (1992, September 24). Criminals are stealing America from us. *The Free Press* (Mankato, MN), p. 5.

Greene, B. (1993, February 11). Naked guy stretches the limits of tolerance. *The Free Press* (Mankato, MN), p. 5.

Greene, B. (1993, March 16). Portable phone junkies deserve an earful. *The Free Press* (Mankato, MN), p. 5.

Greene, B. (1993, March 25). Readers find more reasons to believe. *The Free Press* (Mankato, MN), p. 5.

Greene, B. (1993, April 29). "Why weren't you his friends?" fathers asks. *The Free Press* (Mankato, MN), p. 5.

Greene, M. (1978). *Landscapes of learning.* Columbia University, N.Y.: Teachers College Press.

Green vs. County School Board of New Kent, Virginia. (1968, May 27). 88 SCt 1689, 391 U.S. 430.

Griffin, J. (1993, January 24). U.S. raising generation of abused "time bombs." *Saint Paul Pioneer Press*, p. 11A.

Grow, D. (1993, October 10). Student mediators at Henry High School bring peace—and hope. *Minneapolis Star Tribune*, p. 3B.

Gundlach, S. (1993). Crisis prevention and intervention: Are you prepared? *South Central MN ECSU Review, 5*(1), 10.

Gundlach, S. (1993). Peers helping peers the "natural way." *South Central MN ECSU Review, 5*(1), 11.

Gutek, G. (1983). *Education and schooling in America.* Englewood Cliffs, NJ: Prentice Hall.

Hacker, A. (1992). *Two nations: Black and white, separate, hostile, unequal.* New York: Charles Scribner's Sons.

Haley, A. (1976). *Roots.* Garden City, NY: Doubleday.

Hamburger, T. (1993, December 17). School violence common, data say. *Minneapolis Star Tribune,* pp. 1A, 11A.

Harper, S. (1989, Spring). Resilient kids: Look at the bright side. *School Safety.*

Harrington, W. (1992). *Crossings: A white man's journey into black America.* New York: HarperCollins.

Hawkins, D., Jr., & Doueck, H. (1984). *Social development and the prevention of antisocial behavior among low achievers.* Seattle: National Center for the Assessment of Delinquent Behavior and Its Prevention, School of Social Work, University of Washington.

Healy, M. (1994, May 15). National parks are facing difficult times. *Saint Paul Pioneer Press,* p. 14A.

Hemingway, E. (1932). *Death in the afternoon.* New York: Scribner & Sons.

Hentoff, N. (1993, October 7). Values cut across class lines. *Rocky Mountain News,* p. 48A.

Hepburn scolds "boor" at theater. (1982, March 2). *The Free Press* (Mankato, MN), p. 14.

HHH finds schools major source in uncovering child abuse. (1993, October 25). *Education USA,* p. 2.

Hispanics will soon be largest minority. (1993, September 29). *The Free Press* (Mankato, MN), p. 3.

Hopfensperger, J. (1993, October 29). Experts suggest parenting classes, spiritual guidance. *Minneapolis Star Tribune,* p. 4B.

Hopfensperger, J. (1993, November 5). Seminar awakens teachers to issues of poverty. *Minneapolis Star Tribune,* pp. 1B, 2B.

Hopfensperger, J. (1994, February 20). Not yet 15, they prey on others. *Minneapolis Star Tribune,* p. 18A.

Hundreds show support for black family. (1992, December 26). *The Free Press* (Mankato, MN), p. 13.

Hunger still climbing despite increased charitable efforts. (1993, December 10). *The Leader* (Newsletter of the United Methodist Churches in Minnesota), *10*(26), 11.

Imig, D. (1994). Violence against children. *American Association of Colleges for Teacher Education Briefs, 15*(3), 2.

Ingrassia, M., & McCormick, J. (1994, April 25). Why leave children with bad parents? *Newsweek,* pp. 52–58.

Ivins, M. (1994, April 19). An impulse to be authoritarian. *Minneapolis Star Tribune,* p. 11A.

Jackson, J. (1990, December 1). Black-on-black crime must end. *Minneapolis Star Tribune,* p. 16A.

Jackson, J. (1992, July 14). Democratic national convention. CNN television.

Jefferson, T. (1817). In Beilenson, N. (Ed.). (1986). *His life and words*. White Plains, NY: Peter Pauper Press.

Jewelry stolen from dead bishop is recovered. (1991, June 16). *Sunday Omaha World-Herald*, p. 11A.

Johnson, C., & Johnson, S. (1986). *The one minute teacher*. New York: William Morrow.

Johnson, D., & Johnson, R. (1975). *Learning together and alone*. Englewood Cliffs, NJ: Prentice Hall.

Johnson, D., & Johnson, R. (1991). *Teaching students to be peacemakers*. Edina, MN: Interaction Book Company.

Johnson, D., Johnson, R., Dudley, B., & Burnett, R. (1992). Teaching students to be peer mediators. *Educational Leadership, 50*(1), 10–13.

Jones, J. (1993, October 15). Media perpetuates racism via "Minnesota ice." *Minneapolis Star Tribune*, p. 23A.

Judge scorned, hailed for denying lesbian her child. (1993, September 9). *Saint Paul Pioneer Press*, p. 14A.

Kaplin, M. (1993, December 15). Cutting through the hustle on crime. *Rocky Mountain News* (Denver, CO), p. 72A.

Katz, N., & Lawyer, J. (1993). *Conflict resolution: Building bridges*. Thousands Oaks, CA: Corwin Press.

Kaus, M. (1992). *The end of equality*. New York: Basic Books.

Kelley, C. (1993, August 10). Others have been wrenched from the families they knew. *Minneapolis Star Tribune*, p. 15A.

Kimbrough, R. (1985). *Ethics, a course of study for educational leaders*. Arlington, VA: American Association of School Administrators.

Kimmel, M., & Segel, E. (1983). *For reading out loud!* New York: Delacourte Press.

Kotlowitz, A. (1990). *There are no children here*. New York: Doubleday Dell.

Kozol, J. (November 1992–January 1993). A call to conscience. *SEDLETTER* (Southwest Educational Development Laboratory News), pp. 12–17.

Kramer, M. (1992, May 11). What can be done? *Time*, p. 41.

Kurtines, W., & Gewirtz, J. (1984). *Morality, moral behavior, and moral development*. New York: Wiley.

LaBenne, W., & Greene, B. (1969). *Educational implications of self-concept theory*. Pacific Palisades, CA: Goodyear.

Ladd, G. (1915). *What may I hope?* New York: Longman, Green.

Landers, A. (1993, December 5). Ann recommends book on depression. *Minneapolis Star Tribune*, p. 3E.

Larson, G. (1993, December 29). The Far Side. *Chicago Tribune*, sec. 2, p. 2.

Leonard, P. (1936). In Felleman, H. (Ed.), *The best loved poems of the American people*, (pp. 70–71). Garden City, NY: Doubleday.

Levy, D. (1992, May 11). We have to start talking to each other. *Time*, p. 37.

MacIntyre, A. (1966). *A short history of ethics*. New York: Macmillan.

MacLeod, J. (1987). *Ain't no makin' it: Leveled aspirations in a low-income neighborhood*. Boulder, CO: Westview Press.

Mackenzie, J. (1925). *Manual of ethics*. New York: Nobel & Nobel.

Major, R. (1990). *Discipline: The most important subject we teach*. Lanham, MD: University Press of America.

Man sells violin for $17,000. (1992, March 28). *The Free Press* (Mankato, MN), p. 3.

Man stabbed while helping woman resist subway mugger. (1993, May 15). *St. Cloud Times* (St. Cloud, MN), p. 6A.

Markjarves, G. (1978, November 7). Elderly poor face inflation and loneliness: A reaction to the question asked by all American city judges—"Do you have any poor people and, if so, what do you do with them?" *The Free Press* (Mankato, MN), p. 10.

Marriot, M. (1993, August 20). Some blacks now rip hard-core rap. *Omaha World-Herald*, p. 18.

Marshall, P. (1994). Not right for college? *Better Homes and Gardens, 72*(2), 58–60.

Martin, J. (1991, October 6). Don't meet rudeness with rudeness. *Sunday Omaha World-Herald*, p. 4E.

Mathews, T. (1993, April 26). Looking past the verdict. *Newsweek*, p. 21.

Maxwell, B. (1993, October 11). Reading lifted boy from life of deprivation. *Sunday Omaha World-Herald*, p. 25A.

May, R. (1939). *The art of counseling: How to gain and give mental health.* New York: Abigdon-Cokesbury Press.

Mbitiru, C. (1994, May 16). Rwanda fighting moves closer to seat of temporary government. *Saint Paul Pioneer Press*, p. 2A.

McAdams, R. (1993). *Lessons from abroad: How other countries educate their children.* Lancaster, PA: Technomic Publishing Company.

McCarthy, C. (1993, April 26). Cruel and inhuman punishment. *Minneapolis Star Tribune*, p. 10A.

McCarthy, C. (1992, December 2). If we truly want nonviolence, let's teach it. *Minneapolis Star Tribune*, p. 14A.

McCarthy, C. (1993, August 5). Schools need peace training, not policing. *Minneapolis Star Tribune*, p. 16A.

McCarthy, C. (1993, November 24). Bishops trying to fool the public on sex abuse. *Minneapolis Star Tribune*, p. 13A.

McCullough, D. (1992). *Truman.* New York: Simon & Schuster.

McGinnis, A. (1990). *The power of optimism.* New York: HarperCollins.

McGrory, M. (1993, August 25). Bad idea: Casino as cure for D.C. violence. *Omaha World-Herald*, p. 23.

McWhirter, C. (1993, December 29). 2 children, 2 tragedies: Boy accused of murdering crying infant. *Chicago Tribune*, p. 1.

Meek, M. (1992, Fall). The peacekeepers. *Teaching Tolerance*, pp. 46–52.

Megamall shooting shatters the myth. (1993, February 10). *The Free Press* (Mankato, MN), p. 4.

Meier, P. (1993, April 18). Nurturing fathers needed for boys. *Minneapolis Star Tribune*, pp. 1E, 3E.

Merina, A. (1993). Stopping violence starts with students. *NEA Today, 11*(6), 5–6.

Minnich, H. (1936). *William Holmes McGuffey and his readers.* New York: American Book Company.

Mischke, T. (1993, April 28). Flying bullets at playground show there's no retreat from violence. *Minneapolis Star Tribune*, p. 17A.

Moffat, S. (1992, July 14). L.A. riots ignored and exacerbated Asian's differences. *Saint Paul Pioneer Press*, p. 2A.

Monaghan, G. (1994, January 4). Kids crave community, fear crime. *Minneapolis Star Tribune*, pp. 1E-3E.

Monroe vs. Board of Commonwealth (Comm'rs of City of Jackson, Tennessee). (1968, May 27). 88 SCt 1700, 391 U.S. 450.

Moore, B., & Beland, K. (1992, February 25). *Evaluation of second step, preschool-kindergarten: A violence-prevention curriculum kit.* Seattle: Committee for Children.

Motorist helping abandoned baby assaulted. (1986, January 9). *The Free Press* (Mankato, MN), p. 3.

Moustakas, C. (1967). *Creativity and conformity.* Princeton, NJ: D. Van Nostrand.

Muggers attack woman, take car and money. (1992, July 8). *Saint Paul Pioneer Press*, p. 7B.

Mulkey, Y. (1992). *Character education curriculum.* San Antonio, TX: Character Education Institute.

Myers, D. (1992). *The pursuit of happiness.* New York: Avon Books.

Myrdal, G., Sterner, R., & Rose, A. (1944). *An American dilemma: The Negro problem and modern democracy.* New York: Harper & Brothers.

National Education Association code of ethics. (1976). National Education Association, 1201 16th St. N.W., Washington, DC 20036

National Education Association code of ethics. (1993). National Education Association, 1201 16th St. N.W., Washington, DC 20036.

National killing epidemic sweeps cities. (1992, January 1). *Omaha World-Herald*, p. 8.

Nebraskans to send aid to hurricane victims. (1992, August 29). *Omaha World-Herald*, p. 43.

Newark, NJ, the juvenile automobile theft capitol of the world. (1992, August 12). *WCCO-T.V. News.* 10 P.M.

Nida, E. (1954). *Customs and cultural anthropology for Christian missions.* Pasadena, CA: William Cary Library.

Nonviolence course is a good beginning. (1993, July 12). *Chicago Sun-Times*, p. 21.

"Nude Olympians" spared jail time. (1992, June 3). *The Free Press* (Mankato, MN), p. 5.

Oder, N. (1993, April 11). Trillin plumbs era of optimism in book on friend's suicide. *Minneapolis Star Tribune*, p. 8F.

One in 55 adults on parole, probation or incarcerated. (1987, December 14). *The Free Press* (Mankato, MN), p. 7.

Oppenheimer, D. (1993, September 20). When children fought racist hate: Birmingham church bombing was no random act. *Minneapolis Star Tribune*, p. 13A.

Ornstein, A., & Hunkins, F. (1988). *Curriculum: Foundations, principles, and issues.* Englewood Cliffs, NJ: Prentice Hall.

Oxfam: There's hunger at home. (1992, November 26). *The Free Press* (Mankato, MN), p. 39.

Palermo surgery encouraging. (1993, November 21). *Minneapolis Star Tribune*, p. 2C.

Passenger jet shot down; 28 dead [Sukhumi, Georgia]. (1993, September 22). *The Free Press* (Mankato, MN), p. 3.

Pelton, T. (1994, May 6). Coming soon to a theater near you: Clinton anti-violence message. *Chicago Tribune*, sec. 2, p. 5.

Picone, L. (1993, December 6). The evolving family. *Minneapolis Star Tribune*, p. 11A.

Pitts, L., Jr. (1993, September 26). Outlaw kids: Deep in heart of us, something has gone terribly wrong. *Sunday Omaha World-Herald*, p. 13B.

Plessy vs. Ferguson. (1896, May 18). 16 SCt 1138, 163 U.S. 537.

Police hold 5 youths in golf club attacks. (1987, February 5). *The Free Press* (Mankato, MN), p. 10.

Police link suspect to 200 burglaries. (1987, March 18). *The Free Press* (Mankato, MN), p. 24.

Police say huge scam ring broken. (1993, September 27). *The Free Press* (Mankato, MN), p. 3.

Porter, J. (1993, December 8). Fighting a war on weapons. *Education Week*, 13(14), 24–25.

Possin, K., & Hanson, C. (1993). *Self-defense: A student guide to writing position papers*. Winona, MN: Winona State University.

Potok, A. (1994, January 28). Terrifying trend in Houston. *USA Today*, p. 3A.

Powell, J. (1993, August 21). Gays fear thugs who strike in dark. *Omaha World-Herald*, p. 18.

President Bush calls for "renewed investment in fighting violent street crime." (1992, April). *BJS National Update*, p. 1.

Priest quits after parish won't house AIDS victims. (1992, June 11). *The Free Press* (Mankato, MN), p. 11.

Prince, P. (1993, March 18). School maze: Where to teach homeless kids divides St. Paul and Minneapolis. *Minneapolis Star Tribune*, p. 1B.

Principal suspended in flap over interracial dates. (1994, March 15). *The Free Press* (Mankato, MN), p. 10.

Purpel, D. (1988). *The moral and spiritual crisis in education: A curriculum for justice and compassion in education*. Granby, MA: Bergin & Garvey.

Quake hits India, 50 feared dead [Maharashtra, India]. (1993, September 30). *The Free Press* (Mankato, MN), p 3.

Racial slurs may ban school book. (1994, May 16). *Saint Paul Pioneer Press*, p. 3B.

Rasmussen, J. (1992, July 25). Authorities stand by as abortion foes wage personal terror campaign. *Saint Paul Pioneer Press*, p. 14A.

Raspberry, W. (1993), January 4). To save young men from crime. *Minneapolis Star Tribune*, p. 8A.

Raspberry, W. (1993, May 19) . . . but Peck shouldn't tolerate military life that's unsafe for gays. *Saint Paul Pioneer Press*, p. 11A.

Raspberry, W. (1993, August). Teach values early to reduce numbers of violent youth. *Saint Paul Pioneer Press*, p. 14A.

Raths, L., Harmin, M., & Simon, S. (1966). *Values and teaching: Working with values in the classroom*. Columbus, OH: C. E. Merrill Books.

"Read-Aloud" campaign aimed at increasing reading. (1991, May 20). *The Free Press* (Mankato, MN), p. 3.

Refugees: Cholera feared. (1994, May 7). *The Free Press* (Mankato, MN), p. 1.

Report says children lack legal aid, urges lawyer to volunteer. (1993, August 4). *Minneapolis Star Tribune*, pp. 2A, 4A.

Resilient children and youth share traits that protect them from negative environments. (1992, Winter). *NCREL Clipboard*, (21), p. 7.

Robbers hit church worshippers. (1992, August 26). *The Free Press* (Mankato, MN), p. 3.

Rohter, L. (1992, November 29). Courts beginning to address problems of homeless. *Saint Paul Pioneer Press*, p. 19A.

Roosevelt, E. (1951). In Rawson, H., & Miner, M. (Eds.). (1986). *The New International Dictionary of Quotations*, p. 217. New York: E. P. Dutton.

Rose, C. (1993, January 20). Victim of inconsiderate louts? Don't stand there, talk back. *Saint Paul Pioneer Press*, pp. 1E–2E.

Rosemond, J. (1992). Raising moral children. *Better Homes and Gardens, 70*(12), p. 34.

Rosemond, J. (1993, March). Raising happy kids. *Better Homes and Gardens, 71*(3), p. 44.

Rouillard, L. (1993). *Goals and goal setting.* Menlo Park, CA: Crisp Publications.

Royko, M. (1993, March 26). We don't have to worry, we have programs. *The Free Press* (Mankato, MN), p. 5.

Russell, W. (1984). *Classics to read aloud to your children.* New York: Crown.

Russell, W. (1986). *More classics to read aloud to your children.* New York: Crown.

Ryan, K. (1993). Mining the values in the curriculum. *Educational Leadership, 51*(3), 16–18.

Ryan, M. (1992, March 5). Here, everybody gets to play. *Parade Magazine*, p. 10.

Sagan, C., & Druyan, A. (1994, March 6). Literacy—the path to a more prosperous, less dangerous America. *Parade Magazine*, pp. 4–7.

Salter, S. (1993, August 8). They're promoting random kindness. *Minneapolis Star Tribune*, pp. 1E, 5E.

Santoli, A. (1993, March 28). I like you just the way you are. *Parade Magazine*, pp. 4–5.

Scherer, M. (1992). Solving conflicts—not just for children. *Educational Leadership, 50*(1), 14–18.

Schwarz, J. (1994, January 1). It was a sad time for children who often were victims. *Minneapolis Star Tribune*, pp. 1,14A, 14A.

Scot, W. (1994, May 15). Personality parade. *Parade Magazine*, p. 2.

Seib, G. (1993, October 14). Ignoring the carnage. *The Free Press* (Mankato, MN), p. 4.

Seligman, M. (1990). *Learned Optimism.* New York: Pocket Books, Simon & Schuster.

Seligman, M. (1992, June). "Be an optimist in two weeks." *Self*, p. 32.

Senate approves near-total gift ban. (1994). *The Free Press* (Mankato, MN), p. 1.

Sexual harassment picture distorted by bad definition. (1993, August 18). *Omaha World-Herald*, p. 24.

Sharma, I. (1965). *Ethical philosophy of India.* New York: Harper Torch Books.

Shaver, J., & Strong, W. (1982). *Facing value decisions: Rationale building for teachers.* New York: Teachers College Press, Columbia University.

Shots apparently fired at cars on I-80 near Atlantic. (1992, September 27). *Sunday Omaha World-Herald*, p. 5B.

Sidgwick, H. (1965). *Outlines of the history of ethics.* London: Macmillan.

Silvernail, D. (1985). *Developing positive student self-concept.* Washington, DC: National Education Association.

Simon, S., Howe, L., & Kirschenbaum, H. (1972). *Values clarification: A handbook of practical strategies for teachers and students.* New York: Hart Publishing Company.

Singer, P. (1972, Spring). Famine, affluence, and morality. *Philosophy and Public Affairs, 1*(3), p. 231.

Singer, P. (1972). *Philosophy and public affairs.* Princeton, NJ: Princeton University Press.

Smetanka, M. J. (1993, November 1). New hope for "at-risk" children. *Minneapolis Star Tribune*, pp. 1A, 16A.

Sniper, rock attacks bring warning to avoid section of Florida highway. (1992, November 6). *Minneapolis Star Tribune*, p. 8A.

Snow, M. (1993, May 4). Children pour out fears for future. *Minneapolis Star Tribune*, pp. 1E–3E.

Sprinthall, N., & Sprinthall, R. (1990). *Educational psychology*. New York: McGraw-Hill.

Steinem, G. (1993). *Revolution from within: A book of self-esteem*. Boston: Little, Brown.

Stephens, J. (1993, Winter). A better way to resolve disputes. *School Safety*, pp. 12–14.

Stiles, L., & Johnson, B. (Eds.). (1977). *Morality examined: Guidelines for teachers*, by Barron, W. Princeton, NJ: Princeton Book Company.

Strike, K., & Soltis, J. (1985). *The ethics of teaching*. New York: Teachers College Press, Columbia University.

Students disciplined for anti-Semitism at game. (1993, January 23). *The Free Press* (Mankato, MN), p. 17.

Study finds students have a lot to worry about. (1993, November 24). *Minneapolis Star Tribune*, p. 7A.

Study: Public schools will be one-third minority by 1995. (1991, September 13). *The Free Press* (Mankato, MN), p. 5.

Sullaway, J. (1992, March). Grant's tomb victimized by vandals. *Highways*, p. 12.

Take the high road. (1993, August). An Ethics Booklet for Executive Branch Employees. Washington, DC: GPO.

Tanner, D., & Tanner, L. (1980). *Curriculum development: Theory into practice*. New York: Macmillan.

Tawney, R. (1931). *Equality*. New York: Barnes & Noble.

Taylor, P. (1992, June 21). The invisible dads: More and more are drifting away. *Minneapolis Star Tribune*, p. 21A.

Teacher of the year gives hope to homeless. (1994, April 19). *Minneapolis Star Tribune*, p. 7A.

Teen girl who can't talk enters speech contest. (1992, November 12). *Chicago Tribune*, p. 16.

Teens dropping rocks from overpass kill a man. (1991, July 24). *Omaha World-Herald*, p. 28.

Ten teenage girls accused of jabbing women with pins. (1989, November 5). *Minneapolis Star Tribune*, p. 6A.

Tenenbaum, S. (1947). *Why men hate*. New York: Beechhurst Press.

Terry, W. (1993, February 14). "Make things better for somebody." *Parade Magazine*, pp. 4–5.

Thieves ruining vacations at national parks. (1991, July 22). *The Free Press* (Mankato, MN), p. 3.

Thomas, J. (1993, July). How to be happier: Ten ways to improve your outlook on life. *Better Homes and Gardens*, pp. 66–68.

Thornburgh, D. (1991, January 15). Law and values in a changing world, democracy, law and human rights. *Vital Speeches of the Day*, 57(7), p. 205.

350,000 Germans march against intolerance. (1992, December 7). *Minneapolis Star Tribune*, p. 2A.

Tice, D. (1993, March 3). It's time for American leaders to face a hard issue: Strengthening the family. *Saint Paul Pioneer Press*, p. 8A.

Tiger, L. (1979). *Optimism: The biology of hope*. New York: Simon & Schuster.

Tolstoy, L. (1877). *Anna Karenina*. New York: Barnes & Noble.

Traffic deaths apparently to set 30–year low. (1992, December 30). *The Free Press* (Mankato, MN), p. 5.

Trelease, J. (1989). *The Read Aloud Handbook*. New York: Penguin Books.

Tribal guerrillas gun down 87 people [Manipur, India]. (1993, September 16). *The Free Press* (Mankato, MN), p. 3.

Trillin, C. (1976). Remembering Denny. In Oder, N. (1993, April 11). Trillin plumbs era of optimism in book on friend's suicide. *Minneapolis Star Tribune*, p. 8F.

Troops carry food to irate Floridians. (1992, August 29). *Omaha World-Herald*, p. 1.

Turque, B. (1992, November 23). A new terror on the road. *Newsweek*, p. 31.

20 believed killed by landslide in Sri Lanka. (1993, October 9). *The Free Press* (Mankato, MN), p. 3.

Two charged in snowblower theft. (1993, January 15). *The Free Press* (Mankato, MN), p. 3.

254 crack abusers commit 223,000 crimes. (1989, August 4). *The Free Press* (Mankato, MN), p. 9.

Unruh, G., & Unruh, A. (1984). *Curriculum development: Problems, processes, and progress*. Berkeley, CA: McCutchan.

Usher returns $1,800 to Canterbury patron. (1991, August 5). *The Free Press* (Mankato, MN), p. 5.

Vachss, A. (1993, June 27). Rapists are single-minded sociopathic beasts . . . that cannot be tamed with understanding. *Parade Magazine*, pp. 4, 5.

Vandal strikes at Vietnam Memorial. (1994, March 15). *The Free Press* (Mankato, MN), p. 3.

Vaughan, S. (1988). *The professional development plan*. St. Paul, MN: Minnesota Department of Education.

Violence erupts after canoe race. (1991, April 29). *The Free Press* (Mankato, MN), p. 3.

Violence erupts at Dallas Cowboys' Super Bowl rally. (1993, February 10). *Saint Paul Pioneer Press*, p. 7A.

Violent schools, safe schools: The safe school study report to Congress. (1978). Washington, DC: National Institute of Education.

Vocational Rehabilitation Act. (1973). U.S. Statutes at Large 88 Stat. 1617.

Wallace, C. (1994, April 10). Flogging case has Americans intrigued by Singapore justice. *Minneapolis Star Tribune*, p. 30A.

Wallace, T. (1993, February 14). Make things better for somebody. *Parade Magazine*, p. 4.

Wallach, L. (1993). 4 ways to help children cope with violence. *Education Digest*, 59(2), 29–32.

Walsh, D. (1991, Fall). Antidote for prejudice. *School Safety*, pp. 26–28.

Walsh, J. (1992, August 20). St. Paul educators are urged to build cultural bridges to minority students. *Minneapolis Star Tribune*, p. 5B.

Walsh, J. (1992, December 1). 2 of 3 students say they've been victims. *Minneapolis Star Tribune*, p. 1B.

Walsh, J. (1993, January 5). Robbery victim has a million thanks for high schoolers who came to his aid. *Minneapolis Star Tribune*, p. 5B.

Wangstad, W. (1992, November 6). Cabbie "lucky to be alive" following savage stabbing. *Saint Paul Pioneer Press*, p. 1B.

Wangstad, W. (1994, February 17). Vandals rounded up in Bloomington. *Saint Paul Pioneer Press*, p. 6C.

Ward, G. (1993, June–July). It's not an education if it's value neutral. *Jefferson Center for Character Education* (Pasadena, California).

Warren J. (1993, March 21). A voice for peace. *Chicago Tribune*, sec. 5, p. 2.

Werner, E. (1986). Against the odds. In Harper, S. (1989, Spring). Resilient kids: Look at the bright side. *School Safety*, p. 31.

Wetterling, P. (1993, November 28). Until society decides to protect kids, the abuse will continue. *Minneapolis Star Tribune*, p. 28A.

Wheelis, A. (1974). *The moralist*. Baltimore: Penguin Books.

Wichita abortion doctor wounded. (1993, August 20). *The Free Press* (Mankato, MN), p. 12.

Wiesel, I. (1986, October 27). Those glittering Nobel prizes.*U.S. News & World Report*, p. 68.

Wiesel, E. (1992, April 19). When passion is dangerous. *Parade Magazine*, pp. 20–1.

Will, G. (1992, November 19). These Chicago students learn the art of survival. *The Free Press* (Mankato, MN), p. 4.

Will, G. (1993, March 28). As firearms deviancy shoots higher, nation lowers expectations. *Minneapolis Star Tribune*, p. 23A.

Will, G. (1993, April 15). A dismal "60s-style flashback." *Minneapolis Star Tribune*, p. 26A.

Yates, S. (Ed.). (1994, Spring). Logical link: LRE and violence reduction. *The Legal Circle*, pp. 1, 8.

Youths go on rampage in chic Palm Springs. (1986, March 29). *The Free Press* (Mankato, MN), p. 6.

Zuckerman, M. (1991, October 28). Black and white in America. *U.S. News & World Report*, p. 92.

Index

About the Authors

DEBRA J. ANDERSON is Associate Professor and chair of the Department of Education at St. Olaf College in Northfield, Minnesota.

ROBERT L. MAJOR is Professor in the Department of Curriculum and Instruction at Mankato State University.

RICHARD R. MITCHELL is Professor in the Department of Curriculum and Instruction at Mankato State University.

All three have coauthored *Teacher Supervision that Works: A Guide for University Supervisors* (Praeger, 1992).

ISBN 0-275-94821-8

90000>

EAN

9 780275 948214

HARDCOVER BAR CODE